High Performance

MUZZLELOADING
BIG GAME RIFLES

Stoeger Publishing
Great Outdoor Books & More Since 1924

STOEGER PUBLISHING COMPANY
is a division of Benelli U.S.A.

Benelli U.S.A.
Vice President and General Manager:
  Stephen Otway
Vice President of Marketing and Communications:
  Stephen McKelvain

Stoeger Publishing Company
President: Jeffrey Reh
Publisher: Jay Langston
Managing Editor: Harris J. Andrews
Design & Production Director:
  Cynthia T. Richardson
Photography Director: Alex Bowers
Imaging Specialist: William Graves
National Sales Manager: Jennifer Thomas
Special Accounts Manager: Julie Brownlee
Publishing Assistants:
  Christine Lawton and Tina Talmadge
Administrative Assistant: Shannon McWilliams
Design & Layout: Fatima Taylor
Proofreader: Janet Daniels

Published by Stoeger Publishing Company
17603 Indian Head Highway, Suite 200
Accokeek, Maryland 20607

BK0323
ISBN: 0-88317-268-2
Library of Congress Control Number: 2002115928

Manufactured in the United States of America.

Distributed to the book trade and
to the sporting goods trade by:
Stoeger Industries
17603 Indian Head Highway, Suite 200
Accokeek, Maryland 20607
301-283-6300   Fax: 301-283-6986
www.stoegerpublishing.com

OTHER PUBLICATIONS:
Shooter's Bible
  The World's Standard Firearms
  Reference Book
Gun Trader's Guide
  Complete Fully Illustrated
  Guide to Modern Firearms with
  Current Market Values

Hunting & Shooting:
Advanced Black Powder Hunting
Archer's Bible
Complete Book of Whitetail Hunting
Cowboy Action Shooting
Elk Hunter's Bible
Great Shooters of the World
Hounds of the World
Hunt Club Management Guide
Hunting America's Wild Turkey
Hunting and Shooting
  with the Modern Bow
Hunting Whitetails East & West
Hunting the Whitetail Rut
Labrador Retrievers
The Pocket Survival Guide
Shotgunning for Deer
Taxidermy Guide
Tennessee Whitetails
Trailing the Hunter's Moon
The Turkey Hunter's Tool Kit:
  Shooting Savvy
The Ultimate in Rifle Accuracy
Whitetail Strategies

Collecting Books:
The Lore of Spices
Sporting Collectibles
The Working Folding Knife

Firearms:
Antique Guns
Complete Guide to Modern Rifles
Complete Guide to Service Handguns
Firearms Disassembly
  with Exploded Views
FN Browning Armorer to the World
Gunsmithing at Home
Heckler & Koch:
  Armorers of the Free World
How to Buy & Sell Used Guns
Modern Beretta Firearms
Spanish Handguns
The Ultimate in Rifle Accuracy
The Walther Handgun Story

Reloading:
Complete Reloading Guide
The Handloader's Manual of
  Cartridge Conversions 3rd Ed.
Modern Sporting Rifle Cartridges

Fishing:
Bassing Bible
Catfishing: Beyond the Basics
The Complete Book of Flyfishing
Deceiving Trout
Fishing Made Easy
Fishing Online: 1,000 Best Web Sites
The Fly Fisherman's Entomological
  Pattern Book
Flyfishing for Trout A-Z
The Flytier's Companion
The Flytier's Manual
Handbook of Fly Tying
Ultimate Bass Boats

Cooking Game:
The Complete Book of
  Dutch Oven Cooking
Dress 'Em Out
Fish & Shellfish Care & Cookery
Game Cookbook
Wild About Freshwater Fish
Wild About Game Birds
Wild About Seafood
Wild About Venison
Wild About Waterfowl
World's Best Catfish Cookbook

Wildlife Photography:
Conserving Wild America
Freedom Matters
Wild About Babies

Fiction:
Wounded Moon

CONTENTS

High Performance Muzzleloading Big Game Rifles

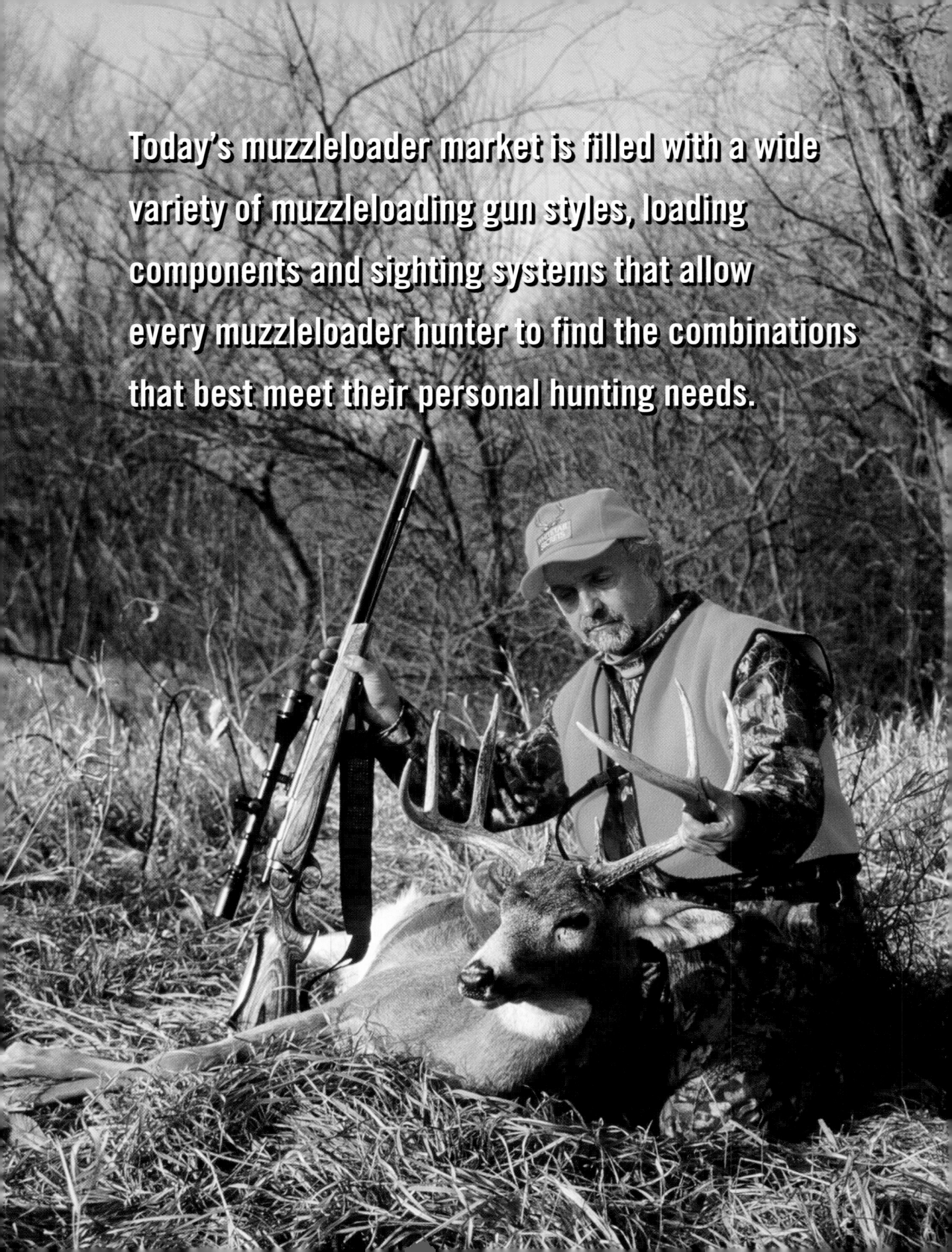

Today's muzzleloader market is filled with a wide variety of muzzleloading gun styles, loading components and sighting systems that allow every muzzleloader hunter to find the combinations that best meet their personal hunting needs.

INTRODUCTION

Muzzleloading has gone ultramodern, and whether you're part of the majority crowd that embraces better muzzleloader performance, or part of the minority that feels muzzleloading has gotten way too modern, the sport has changed. It's not showing any signs of going back to its old ways. In fact, muzzleloader hunting is now more performance driven than at anytime in history.

Many of today's newer muzzle-loaded big game rifles are every bit as advanced as any center-fire cartridge rifle currently available, and when it comes to accuracy, many of them will now shoot right along with the center-fires out to 200 yards. Ballistically, at the muzzle and downrange, some of the hotter loads fired by these front-loading wonders will surpass the performance of older deer cartridges, like the .30-30 Winchester or the .35 Remington. Some even match the hard-hitting performance of cartridges like the venerable .35 Whelen or .444 Marlin. Simply put, today's modern in-line ignition high performance muzzleloading big game rifles, loaded with hunting projectiles of the same advanced technology are now fully capable of delivering minute-of-angle accuracy with significantly increased knockdown power.

Why Hunt with a Modern Muzzleloader?

Nostalgia plays a reduced role in why a modern-day hunter would turn to a slow-to-load front-loaded rifle for pursuing big game. Those shooters and hunters who have gotten into muzzleloading in order to relive history and experience what it was like to hunt with a traditional flintlock or percussion rifle style dating from the 1700s or early 1800s now represent a distinct minority. Less than 10 percent of all muzzle-loaded guns sold today are old-fashioned side-hammer designs.

The growth in the number of muzzleloading hunters in the United States and Canada can be directly linked to the growth of North America's big game populations. Just about everywhere, muzzleloading big game seasons have become yet another management tool for game departments faced with the task of balancing wildlife populations with available suitable habitat. And these special muzzleloader hunts now represent an honest "third season" opportunity to hunt deer and other big game. With only a few exceptions, just about every state and Canadian province now offers the serious big game hunter separate seasons in which to hunt with modern firearm…bow and arrow…and muzzleloader.

ABOVE: At one time, the lure of the muzzleloading seasons was to experience what it was like to hunt with a front-loader of old-fashioned design, to relive a bit of history. Today, they are for both the muzzleloading historian as well as the serious big game hunter looking for more time in the field each fall.

FAR LEFT: Muzzleloading has gone hi-tech, and today's new breed of muzzleloading hunter is looking for all of the accuracy, range and knockdown power possible from a front-loaded big game rifle. Author Toby Bridges is shown here with a custom "smokeless" muzzleloading big game rifle.

Those who hunt with muzzle-loaded guns of traditional design now represent less than 10 percent of all hunters who participate in the special muzzleloader seasons or hunts.

Hunters are taking to the special muzzleloading big game seasons in record numbers. It is estimated that there are now 3.5 million muzzleloading shooters in the United States. And today's average muzzleloading shooter is a muzzleloading hunter who is looking for a little modern technology to ensure that when the smoke clears, the game will be laying on the ground. Whether or not there's actually smoke hanging in the air doesn't seem to matter much these days. The game-taking performance of the rifle carried afield is now far more important than whether or not the muzzleloader is of authentic style. The rifles and loads now favored coast to coast are a far cry from the long-barreled Kentucky rifle that Daniel Boone carried westward 200 years ago.

Modern Changes

The front-loading big game rifle of choice these days is a very modern in-line percussion rifle with many of the same features found on bolt-action center-fire hunting rifles. Close to 80 percent of all muzzleloading guns sold annually are now of in-line ignition design. As a rule, these rifles display extremely modern rifle lines, are short and fast handling, weigh considerably less than muzzleloaders of the past, feature a receiver that's drilled and tapped for quick and easy scope mounting, and come equipped with a convenient safety that allows these muzzleloaders to be carried cocked and ready for action. Many of today's top-selling models are now even built with a "bolt-action" receiver. In fact, Remington, Ruger and Savage offer bolt-action models that feature a receiver that is very similar to the actions found on their cartridge models.

Just as modern as the rifles carried during today's special muzzleloader seasons are the loading components with which they are stuffed. Shooting real black powder has almost become a thing of the past. First introduced back in 1975, Pyrodex had become the most widely used muzzleloading propellant by the time the early in-line rifles began to show up during the mid- to late 1980s. Produced by Hodgdon Powder Company, the propellant was officially classified as "smoke-less propellant," even though it had been specially formulated for use in muzzle-loaded guns and produced basically the same pressures as black powder, which has always been classified as an "explosive." The "smokeless" classification meant that Pyrodex could be stored on dealers' shelves, could be more easily shipped and did not require the paperwork involved in the sale of black powder. A muzzle-loading shooter could purchase powder for his front-loaded rifle much easier, and with fewer restrictions.

Now we have a relatively new Hodgdon produced black powder substitute known as Triple Seven. The powder, introduced in 2002, is quickly replacing Pyrodex since the new propellant delivers considerably better ballistics with the same load. Plus Triple Seven is formulated without sulfur, which greatly reduces the corrosive nature of the residue left behind when a charge burns.

During the spring of 2000, Savage Arms Company became the first to introduce a muzzleloader designed…engineered…and built to be loaded and shot with modern nitrocellulose-based smokeless powders. With 40- to 45-grain loads of powders like IMR-4227, Accurate Arms XMP5744, and VihtaVuori N110, the company's Model 10ML II holds the distinction of being the first (and only at the time this book was published) front-loaded big game rifle for use with these cleaner burning and non corrosive powders. It is also the only .50 caliber muzzleloader capable of pushing a saboted 250-grain bullet at velocities exceeding 2,300 f.p.s.—and with more than 3,000 foot-pounds of big-game-taking energy.

New Bullets Perform Better

The type of hunting projectile favored by the modern-day muzzleloading hunter has changed dramatically over the past 20 years. Through the 1970s, the biggest debate among muzzleloading shooters and the slowly growing ranks of muzzleloader hunters revolved around the type of projectile. Those who favored muzzleloading rifle designs from before to just after 1800 almost always opted for the patched round ball. On the other hand, modern gun hunters making the move into muzzleloading tended to favor the big and heavy soft lead bore-sized conical bullets for their increased knockdown power.

In 1984, shooters and hunters were offered a third choice—jacketed hand-gun bullets gripped by a plastic sabot. Introduced by a small northern Arkansas company known as Muzzleload Magnum Products, the sabot system was to do as much for the modernization of muzzleloader hunting as the introduction of the in-line ignition rifles. While there have been significant improvements in bore-sized conical bullets over the past 25 years, more muzzleloading hunters today rely on a saboted bullet than those who use a patched round ball or heavy lead conical combined.

Until the late 1990s, fans of the sabot system were faced with the task of loading an undersized modern pistol bullet into a larger diameter bore using a tough plastic sabot cup. To ensure good expansion and transfer of energy, the majority of hunters favored jacketed hollow-point bullets. Those who preferred .50 caliber rifles could choose between .44 caliber (.429 to .430) bullets or .45 caliber (.451 to .452) projectiles, using the appropriate sabot. The wide selection of these bullets available from companies like Hornady, Speer, Nosler and Sierra permit hunters to load and shoot bullet weights ranging from as light as 180 grains all the way up to more than 300 grains. The sabot system's popularity skyrocketed since it allowed the hunter to tailor a load for the game being hunted.

Hunters soon found the saboted bullets far superior to the older, pure lead projectiles. The only fault many performance-minded hunters found with the system was the poor aerodynamics of the blunt-nosed hollow-point bullets. The design of these projectiles tends to slow them down out past 100 yards, reducing retained energy levels and adding considerably to the drop at extended ranges.

Fortunately, that's the way it use to be. A number of bullet makers now market an ever growing selection of bullets that have been designed specifically for shooting with a sabot out of today's high performance muzzleloading big game rifles. Many of these bullets feature a considerably higher ballistic coefficient for vastly improved downrange performance. Some of the newer

As many as 3.5 million shooters and hunters in the United States now own muzzleloading guns. Today's muzzleloading shooter is a hunter looking for bonus hunting opportunities.

Game departments are discovering that the special muzzleloader hunting seasons can also be utilized as another effective game mangement tool, especially for burgeoning whitetail populations in a growing number of states.

TOP: High performance muzzleloading big game rifles, like the Savage Model 10ML II used by the author here, are now delivering unbelievable game-taking performance.

BOTTOM: The scoped Knight thumbhole-stocked "Wolverine" carried by this hunter was once illegal in nearly 80 percent of the states. Now such technology can be used during the vast majority of the special muzzleloader hunts.

spire-point or spitzer style saboted bullets are capable of delivering 300 to 600 foot-pounds of additional knockdown energy at 200 yards over a blunt-nosed hollow-point bullet of the same weight that left the muzzle at the same velocity. A more aerodynamic design improves accuracy and flattens trajectory.

When the time is taken to properly match bullet and sabot with an optimum powder charge, today's high-quality fast-twist barrels are capable of punching tight 100-yard groups that rival those shot with a top-of-the-line bolt-action .270 Winchester or 7mm Remington Magnum center-fire. In fact, this outstanding performance has continued to keep modern muzzle-loaded big game rifles under fire from the diminishing ranks of hunters with a traditional mind-set.

Dissension within the Ranks

Even before the first Knight MK-85 in-line rifles and Muzzleload Magnum Products sabots hit the market, muzzleloading shooters were already bickering among themselves. Generally, these often heated debates centered on the authenticity of the reproduction guns and loads being shot. It was, however, the introduction of the modern in-line and plastic saboted bullets that caused traditional shooters and hunters to put aside their petty differences and fight to get the modern guns and loads outlawed during the special muzzleloader hunting seasons.

Many claimed that the vastly improved performance of today's high-tech muzzleloaders, telescopic sights and saboted jacketed bullets would cause game departments to eliminate the special seasons. Now, ask yourself... "Have we lost one single muzzleloading season to such technology?"

No, we haven't. In fact, the improved performance of the modern in-line rifles, the better ballistics possible with today's powders and improved bullet designs, plus the acceptance of telescopic sights during the majority of the present muzzleloader seasons have had just the opposite effect. All of these things have encouraged new participants to join the ranks of muzzleloader hunters in just about every state. In turn, this growth has encouraged game departments to expand muzzleloader hunting opportunities.

Keep in mind that when many of the early "muzzleloader only" seasons were established during the 1960s and '70s, the white-tailed deer populations in many states were just beginning to recover from all-time low levels. Game departments were concerned about over-harvesting and deer hunting regulations were very restrictive. Now these same agencies are finding themselves on the other side of the fence. In many parts of the country there are now too many deer, and bag limits have become quite liberal. To encourage additional harvest, game departments have established new seasons, including separate muzzleloader hunting seasons. These departments have discovered that muzzleloading seasons have become yet another effective game management tool.

Change Is Inevitable

The antiquated muzzleloading regulations still found in a few states that require hunters to head out with anything less than the most effective rifle, load and sighting system are the result of pressure from, of all things, state muzzleloading organizations. It is unfortunate, but most such organizations are almost totally made up of shooters who have gotten into the sport for the sake of participating in old-fashioned shooting matches. Some of these muzzleloader fanciers don't even hunt, but game departments and regulators listen to them and these shooters tend to oppose the modernization of this sport.

What muzzleloader hunting needs is a strong national organization with the resources and backbone to stand up to the historical shooting organizations. Modern firearms big game hunters have the Safari Club International and the Boone & Crockett Club, while bowhunters have their Pope & Young Club to represent their hunting interests. All muzzleloading has are a couple of very fragmented organizations, but nothing with the clout to get much of anything accomplished.

Not all is bleak for the modern muzzleloading hunter. The muzzleloader regulations now found in the majority of states today are broad enough to pretty well allow the hunter to use the style of rifle, powder, projectile and type of sights he or she prefers. Also, today's market is filled with a wide variety of muzzleloading gun styles, loading components and sighting systems that allow every muzzleloader hunter to find the combinations that best meet their hunting needs.

High Performance Muzzleloading Big Game Rifles

Most hunters dream about a hunt for a great bull elk like that taken here by Jimmy Primos, of Primos Hunting Calls. When and if they get that chance, they don't leave anything to chance with the muzzleloading rifle and load they carry. They simply want the performance to get the job done.

Through the years there have been scores of good books written and published about loading, shooting and hunting with muzzleloaders in general. Those of you who are now mostly interested in the performance of the latest muzzleloaded rifles, and that is the majority of today's muzzleloader owners, have had to wade through chapters covering everything from "Mastering the Flintlock" to "Rendezvousing" in hopes of finding bits of information that might help you get better accuracy, more knockdown power or more reliable ignition with your modern in-line hunting rifle. Well, here's the book you've been waiting for.

In the pages of High Performance Muzzleloading Big Game Rifles you'll find everything you'll need to take any new in-line muzzleloading big game rifle from the box to photos of you with the buck or bull of a lifetime. We'll cover all aspects of getting top performance from any of these rifles, including working up loads, choosing the best projectile, proper scope selection, coping with muzzleloader trajectory, understanding downrange performance, tips for maintaining accuracy during the heat of summer or the cold of winter, field maintenance for the modern in-line rifle, plus much, much more.

—Toby Bridges, Author

the evolution of
FIREPOWER

For most of the nearly seven centuries that muzzleloading guns have been around, the continued development of front-loaded arms has been driven by two quests—to make ignition systems more reliable and sure-fire, and to improve the knockdown power of these slow-to-load guns. As much as most hunters would like to think that the evolution of muzzle-loaded guns came about because of their sporting needs, the truth is improvements to early muzzleloaders were made to enhance their reliability and devastation on the battlefield. The hunter simply benefited from all of this refinement.

The first hand-held firearms appeared in Europe during the 1300s. The exact country of origin or date are not known. But early military documents of the late 14th Century regularly make mention of muzzle-loaded firearms known as hand cannons. These were simple metal tubes, often cast bronze or iron, that were commonly attached to the end of a "lance-like" pole. In use, the loaded hand cannon (and pole) were held under one arm, somewhat aimed at the opposing force, then fired by igniting a small amount of priming powder that had been poured over a small "touch hole" near the top rear center of the small cannon. Fire for ignition was usually provided by a slow-burning nitrated rope, known as a match.

Even a small hand cannon regularly sported a bore approaching an inch across. Into this, the shooter would pour in an undetermined amount of crude, early black powder, then a projectile was either simply dropped in or helped down the bore with a short ramrod. Historians have determined that often the projectile used would generally be dictated by the soldier's surroundings. Surely they used early cast bronze or iron, maybe even lead balls that were close to the diameter of the small hand-held cannon, but these early muzzleloaders were also known to be fired with nothing more than a rock as the projectile.

Now, these were for the most part crude forged or cast metal tubes, closed at one end. It probably did not take many rounds before the shooter realized that more powder also meant more recoil, or whatever they called it back then. Likewise, it is a good bet that many of these earliest muzzle-loaded guns burst from being overloaded. Still, with these early hand cannons, muzzleloading and firearms had been born.

By the early 1400s, the natural evolution that can only be brought about by the use of anything resulted in hand-ignited arms fitted with a stock that allowed the arm to be fired from the shoulder, and to be haphazardly aimed. An improve-

FAR LEFT: The long-barreled "Pennsylvania" or "Kentucky" rifles, which were distinctly American in design, made more efficient use of powder and lead than large-bore European rifles. The longer barrel allowed a more complete burn of the powder charge, producing higher velocities.

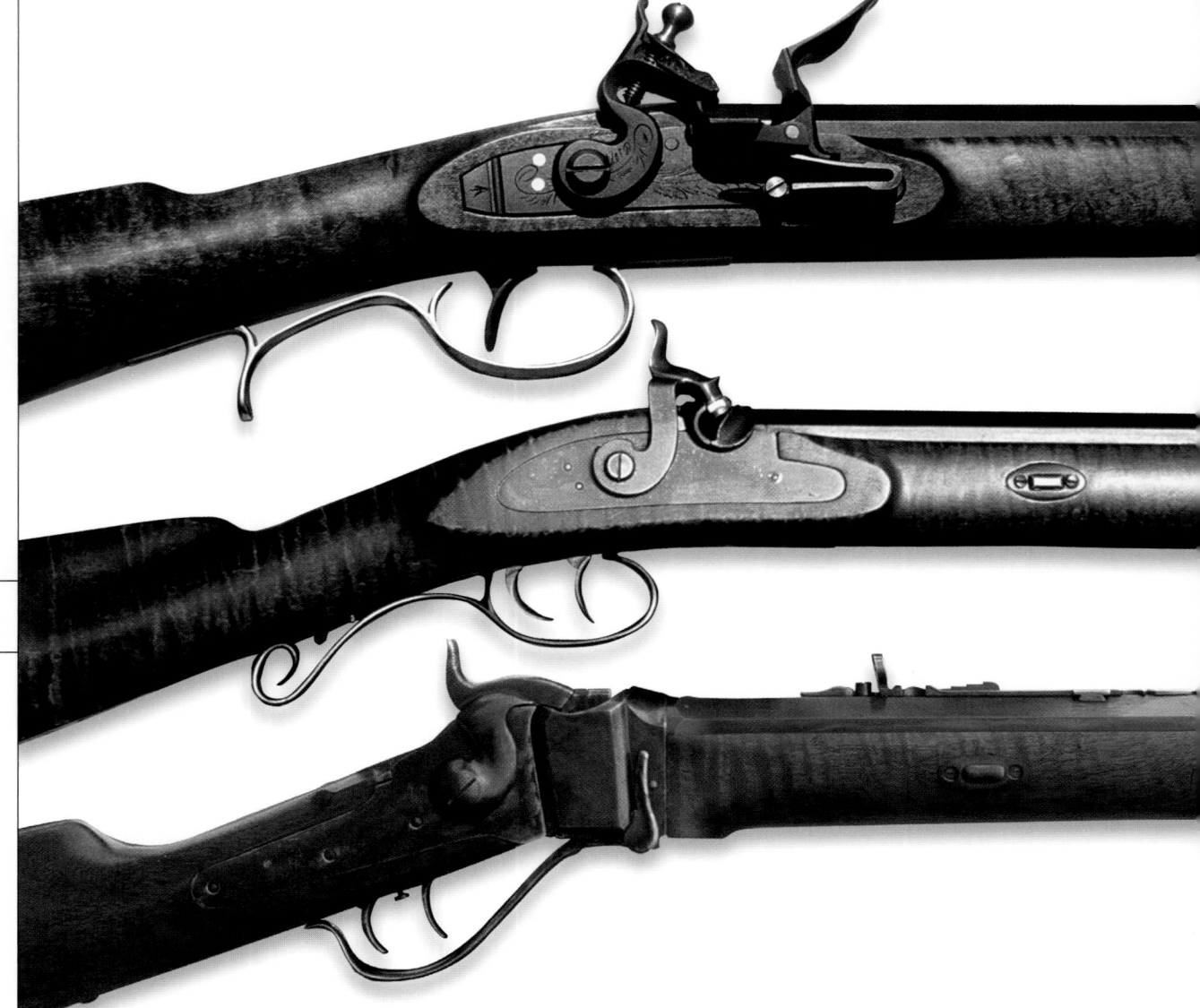

TOP: The true flintlock, developed during the early 1600s, is considered to be the first true "hunter's muzzleloader." The mechanism could produce its own fire for ignition, and was simple enough in design that even a backwoods gunsmith could repair or replace internal and external parts.

CENTER: One of the more popular "working rifles" of settlers headed west, as well as the hardy breed of adventurers known as "mountain men," was the big half-stock "Hawken" rifle. These rifles were commonly of .52 or .54 caliber, stoked with massive powder charges.

BOTTOM: The percussion ingnition system only saw widespread use for about 50 years, and was replaced by early cartridge guns like this big .50/70 Sharps "Old Reliable."

ment of the stocked hand cannon became known as the matchlock, which held the burning match in an S-shaped lever attached to one side of the gun. This allowed the shooter to do a better job of aiming, and then lever the match down into the priming powder when ready to shoot. And it was probably with one of these early 15th-Century arms that the very first hunter took the very first head of big game with a muzzleloader.

By the end of that century, many refinements had been made to the matchlock. Most importantly, some ingenious early gunsmith came up with the first truly mechanical ignition system when the match became held by a spring-powered hammer that could be mechanically dropped into the priming charge when a trigger was pulled. To allow for better aiming, the priming charge was now held in a shallow pan-like arrangement located at the side of the barrel. Military firepower had just become far more sophisticated.

The first ignition system that could produce its own fire for ignition was introduced during the early 1500s. Again, the origin of the wheellock is not truly known, but some say the first such guns were either built in Germany or Italy. As the name suggests, the wheellock incorporated a serrated, hardened steel wheel located adjacent to the priming pan. This wheel could be "cocked" by a spanner wrench, then mechanically locked in place by an early form of sear. Power for the wheel was provided by a very intricate internal spring-powered mechanism. And once the wheel had been turned and locked in place, a movable arm could be positioned to press a small piece of pyrite against the serrations of the wheel. When the trigger was pulled, the wheel was released and sparks would fly. And, hopefully, the priming charge in the pan would ignite and set off the powder charge in the barrel.

Wheellock ignition arms were extremely difficult and time consuming to build. Likewise, they were extremely expensive, and became the arms of the rich and nobility, who used them for hunting all of the big game of Europe. The guns were also very prone to mechanical failure and breakage of internal parts. Because of their high rate of mechanical problems, they were never widely used. The military powers of the time continued to use the easier to maintain matchlock, right up until the development of the flint and steel ignition system during the 17th Century.

The flintlock first appeared in cruder form as the German snaphaunce and Spanish miquelet, which placed some mechanical parts on the outside of the lock plate and relied on iron pyrite striking a serrated or grooved frizzen for producing the sparks needed to ignite the priming powder. Some of these early versions of the flintlock also relied on a two-piece frizzen and pan cover, requiring that the pan cover be moved out of the way before the gun could be fired.

The true flintlock, utilizing a one-piece frizzen and pan cover, is generally considered to have been developed in France during the early 1600s. Gunmakers continued to refine this ignition system for more than 200 years, and the flint ignition systems being used at the turn of the 19th Century were some of the finest muzzleloader lock mechanisms ever produced. Even so, from the first true flintlock systems, all relied on basically the same mechanical concept for producing the desired effect—the ignition of the priming charge in the pan and the firing of the front-loader.

If everything was right, including the weather conditions, this was accomplished when the trigger was pulled and the hammer fell, causing a sharp-edged piece of flint to strike the hardened surface of the frizzen.

Then, as the hammer continued its forward and downward movement, the sharp edge of the flint scraped away a minute amount of steel from the frizzen, resulting in a shower of sparks. As the frizzen moved forward from the hammer strike, the bottom portion that formed the pan cover lifted and exposed the small charge of fine black powder priming. And if the sparks produced were hot enough, the shooter had ignition.

The flintlock was the first true hunter's gun. The internal mechanisms were so simple, many wilderness gunmakers in the American colonies were able to hand forge every part needed to build a lock, or to repair one that had seen hard use. The system allowed the hunter to carry his rifle already cocked and ready for use when making the final stalk on deer or other big game. And when the trigger was pulled, there was a high probability that the muzzleloader would fire.

The flintlock reigned far longer than the percussion ignition system that replaced the flint and steel system. Fortunately, with the percussion ignition system we have a name to associate with its development, Reverend Alexander Forsyth. Fortunately, this English religious leader was also something of an amateur chemist and a hunter.

Westward travelers were often faced with harvesting game larger than the common whitetail of the East, and quickly recognized the need for larger bore muzzleloading rifles with more knockdown power.

As crude as the big "flintlock" of this early Indian trade gun may seem, ignition of this type was the first true practical muzzleloading ignition system for the hunter.

Forsyth had grown tired of how the flash of the pan from his flintlock fowler would often spook the geese and swans he hunted for both sport and food for the table. He had been studying the explosive nature of fulminate of mercury and found ways of containing the fire to produce more consistent and spontaneous ignition for muzzleloading guns. His work with the fulminate led to the introduction of the percussion ignition system as early as 1805. One of the earliest known percussion systems was known as the "scent bottle" system, and relied on a tiny "pill" of fulminate that was contained inside a bottle-shaped chamber on the side of the barrel. When the hammer struck a plunger, that, in turn, struck the fulminate inside the chamber, fire passed through the vent or flash channel and into the powder charge.

It wasn't until the actual invention of the percussion cap and nipple that the newly designed system began to win favor with shooters and hunters. The invention of the percussion cap can also be credited to another Englishman, Joshua Shaw. He completed the development of his idea in 1813 while still living in England. However, he did not release his design until making the move to the United States, where he applied for and received a patent in 1814. Shaw's original design does not differ all that much from the No. 11 percussion caps still used today. (It should be noted that is was within only a couple of years after the introduction of the percussion cap that the first true in-line percussion ignition designs were developed.)

Bigger Is Better

Since the earliest military use of muzzle-loaded firearms, and on through the end of the Civil War, military leaders realized that to deliver the lethal blow needed to put an enemy soldier down required the use of a relatively large bore. Until the refinement of the easy-loading conical Minié Bullet of the mid-1800s, the round ball had remained as the military projectile for more than 500 years. Bores of around .70 to .75 caliber, loaded with round ball projectiles weighing 500 to 600 grains, were more the rule than the exception. Even when major military forces began to switch to rifled-muskets and elongated bullets, their old way of thinking still dictated bores of .577 or .58 caliber, and bullets weighing around 500 grains.

Early muzzleloading big game hunters in Europe and Great Britain were really never all that far from sources for black powder or lead for making into round balls. Some of the larger game being hunted included wild boar that could top 500 pounds, red stag that could top that, and European brown bears that might weigh 700 or more pounds. The muzzle-loaded hunting rifles of European nobility through the 1600s and into the early 1800s commonly had bores running from .62 to .75 caliber, made to shoot massive amounts of black powder behind the heavy round balls to produce the energy needed to cleanly down really large game.

When the early European settlers came to America, the gunmakers that moved here with them first began to produce arms that were very similar to those in use back in Europe. The guns often sported relatively short (32- to 36-inch) barrels, and the same huge bores that were popular in their homeland. However, as settlers began to spread farther and farther away from large established population centers, the sources for powder and lead were far and few between. Rifle makers were faced with a new challenge—to come up with a new breed of muzzleloading rifle that did a more efficient job with lighter powder charges and smaller, lighter round balls.

Out of this need to conserve came the long-barreled rifles that became distinctively American in design. Often referred to as Pennsylvania or Kentucky rifles, the new domestically built front-loaders often sported barrels that were 40 to 44 inches in length, and bore sizes had shrunk to .40 to .44 caliber. While these rifles still would not produce the same energy levels as a .62 caliber German jaeger loaded with 120 grains of black powder behind a 325- to 340-grain soft lead ball, the smaller bored American longrifles shot a lighter 90- to 130-grain ball at much higher velocities. And in the hands of an expert rifleman, the rifles would deliver all the knockdown power needed to take even deer-sized game at 100 yards—or drop an enemy at the same distance. And another advantage of such a small bore is that it could be loaded with a light powder charge and used to take small game like squirrels, rabbits or wild turkey without completely destroying edible meat.

As the East became more settled, and loading components became easier to acquire, American hunters also began to favor slightly larger bores. During the early 1800s, it was easier and less costly to have an older original flintlock rifle

The longer barrel and smaller .38 to .44 caliber bore of an eastern "longrifle" made more efficient use of black powder charges than the huge .60 to .75 caliber guns European settlers brought with them to America.

converted to the new and more reliable percussion ignition system than to have a whole new rifle built. Also, an older gun that may have been in service for 30 or 40 years could have a bore that was shot out. Again, it was a lot less costly to have a riflesmith rebore the old barrel to a larger caliber and cut sharp new rifling than to have a whole new barrel hammer forged. Many rifles that started life as a .40 to .44 caliber ended up as rifles of .47 to .52 caliber. And when hunters began to stoke the rifles with heavier powder charges and heavier, larger diameter round balls, they also realized just how much more effective the guns were on big game.

By the time the West was being explored, rifles of .52 to .54 caliber were becoming more widely used, especially by those who might find themselves face to face with a grizzly bear or the task of harvesting a 2,000-pound buffalo to feed a hungry family or wagon train headed for the Pacific coast. Two brothers in St. Louis became famous for the rugged big-bore muzzleloading half-stock rifles they turned out—Samuel and Jacob Hawken. While they did build a few .40 to .45 caliber rifles for local use in the Midwest, most of the guns they built were .50 caliber and larger. And the guns were designed to shoot tremendous 120- to 150-grain powder charges.

With an adequate load of black powder and a proper fitting patched round ball, modern reproduction muzzleloaders can deliver enough knockdown power for taking big game at 50 to 75 yards.

During the early 1800s, British sportsmen discovered the "Dark Continent"—and the wealth of big game to be hunted there. Some of it the biggest game on earth, such as elephant and rhinos. Many of the early hunters headed for Africa took with them huge, heavy rifles of 2- and 4-bore. (A 2-bore rifle has a bore size of 1.325", while the "smaller" 4-bore measures a mere 1.052" across inside the bore.) These guns were loaded and shot with as much as 300 grains of black powder behind a ball that weighed 1,200 to 1,400 grains! Such loads were fully capable of delivering one of those huge balls with 4,000+ foot-pounds of energy for taking game that might weigh 10,000 pounds. Fortunately, those rifles were also very heavy, usually tipping the scales at 20 or more pounds—or they could have killed on both ends.

With the refinement of elongated conical bullets for muzzleloading rifles from around 1830 to 1860, shooters and hunters quickly discovered they could actually produce higher killing energy with a smaller bore rifle. Bores of .40 to .45 caliber were once again in vogue. But instead of being loaded with a light sphere of lead that weighed 90 to 130 grains, these new bullet rifles were shot with long cylindrical bullets that could weigh from 300 to 500 grains. And with 70 to 100 grains of black powder, the rifles were capable of generating energy levels twice or more than that of a rifle of the same caliber loaded with a patched round ball.

When muzzleloading experienced a rebirth during the 1960s and '70s, it didn't take modern-day hunters long to discover the benefits of hunting with a conical bullet. The 20th-Century hunter quickly became impressed with the higher energy levels produced by modern conical designs like the Thompson/Center Arms "Maxi-Ball," the Lee Precision R*E*A*L* Bullet (Rifling Engraved At Loading) and the Buffalo Bullet Company bullets.

After a decade or so of shooting mostly the round ball out of the modern-made reproduction muzzleloading guns of the late 1950s and '60s, harder-hitting bore-sized conical lead bullets replaced the patched ball as the most widely used muzzleloader hunting projectile—for the second time in history.

With the introduction of the modern in-line ignition rifles, and faster twist bores, during the mid-1980s, muzzleloading hunters slowly began to abandon the heavy lead bore-sized conical in favor of a brand-new projectile system built with a modern jacketed pistol bullet gripped by a plastic sabot. The concept allowed the hunter to choose from a much wider range of projectiles, allowing hunting loads to be better tailored for the size of game being hunted. And out of the new in-line rifles some of the loads shot would shoot as accurately as many center-fire big game rifles at 100 yards.

Muzzleloading today has become more performance driven than at any other time in history. And that's because it is now a hunting sport, and the majority of the estimated 3.5 million muzzleloading hunters found in North America strive to shoot the fastest, flattest shooting, hardest-hitting and most accurate powder charge and bullet that's currently available. And some

Author Toby Bridges, shown here in the early 1980s, combined a bit of tradition and a bit of modern technology to build this custom half-stock big game rifle, installing a fast-twist rifling barrel for superior accuracy with a hard-hitting conical bullet.

of today's hotter in-line rifles loaded with maximum or near maximum loads are fully capable of generating better game-taking performance than many of the center-fire cartridge rifles hunters use during the general firearms seasons. And because of the significantly improved performance of today's high performance muzzleloading big game rifles, more and more shooters are using their frontloaders for all of their big game hunting, even during seasons where they could shoot a rifle of center-fire cartridge design.

The patched round ball hunting loads used by American longrifle shooters of about 1800 would get a 90- to 130-grain ball out of the muzzle of a 40-inch barreled .40 to .45 caliber rifle at about 1,800 f.p.s., which is good for around 800 to 900 foot-pounds of energy—at the muzzle. Even the big .54 caliber half-stock plains rifles of the 1840s, with a 120-grain charge of FFg black powder, would only get a 230 grain ball out of the muzzle at around 1,800 f.p.s. However, due to the heavier weight of the larger ball, the load generated close to 1,600 f.p.e. With some of today's more advanced in-line rifle models, it's not uncommon for a maximum load to push a saboted 250-grain jacketed spire-point bullet from the muzzle at 2,200 to 2,300 f.p.s. That translates into 2,650 to 2,950 foot-pounds of big game knockdown power—Now, we're talking real firepower!

modern reproduction
FRONT-LOADING
RIFLES

FAR RIGHT: For many, the lines and looks of a traditional rifle are still appealing. Some modern day hunters have taken to side-hammer rifles of hybrid styling, like the Traditions' "Buckskinner Carbine," with traditional styling and a fast-twist sabot-shootin' bore.

Less than 10 years after the very first of what was to become known as a "reproduction" muzzleloading rifle hit the U.S. market, the needs of the modern-day muzzleloading hunter began to dictate the need for a bore large enough for cleanly taking big game. When the late Turner Kirkland, founder of Dixie Gun Works, traveled to Belgium in 1955 to seek out a gun-maker that would tackle the job of producing a completely modern-made muzzleloader of mid-1800s design, thoughts of producing a front-loaded rifle that was suitable for hunting deer and other big game had never even entered his mind. He was there to bring to American shooters a safe and reliable muzzleloading rifle that was suited more to punching holes in target paper than game.

An avid collector of "Kentucky" rifles, Kirkland took with him a list of the features that were most common to the more than 100 originals in his collection. The average bore size of these rifles was right at .40 caliber, and when the Dixie New Squirrel Rifle first appeared in the Dixie Gun Works catalog in 1956, in both flint and percussion ignition, the rifle was offered in .40 caliber. While the bore of this rifle was actually too small for big game and too large for small game, the .40 caliber bore was welcomed by the then growing number of muzzleloading target shooters simply looking for a new-made muzzleloader built with a modern steel barrel and a lock mechanism that wasn't worn out from 100 years of hard use. Most importantly, the Dixie reproduction muzzle-loaded rifle marked the beginning of a new industry, and the beginning of a new era for muzzleloading popularity.

Beginning of the .45 Caliber Reign

For the hunter among the growing ranks of muzzleloading shooters nationwide, it was a natural urge to tackle the challenge of taking game with a slow-to-load front-loaded rifle. Serious muzzleloading big game hunters through the late 1950s and early 1960s either used a reconditioned original with a larger .45, .50 or .54 caliber bore, or they went to the trouble and expense of building or having built a custom rifle of a suitable bore size. It quickly became apparent to a still infant reproduction muzzleloading gun industry that there was the need for rifles that could deliver adequate punch to bring down big game.

In 1963, Dixie Gun Works upped the bore size of the New Squirrel Rifle to

.45 caliber. And it was that year the author purchased one of the rifles…specifically for hunting deer in my home state of Illinois. I still remember the fun of getting out and shooting…and shooting…and shooting that rifle until I had worked up a good load that shot accurately out to 100 yards, and which I felt confident would do the job on deer-sized game. I was just 14 years old at the time. And that first year hunting with the rifle, in Illinois and next door in Missouri, I managed to take a pair of eight-point bucks—and I've been hunting with muzzleloaders ever since.

The load I settled on was 70 grains of FFFg black powder behind a tightly patched .440" round ball that weighed right at 128 grains. Out of the 40-inch barrel, the load was good for right at 1,900 f.p.s. However, due to the light weight of the .440" round ball, the load developed just 1,025 f.p.e. at the muzzle. And by the time that tiny sphere of soft lead reached 100 yards, it retained only about 300 foot-pounds of energy. I wouldn't even think about hunting deer with such a load today, but back when I was a skinny teenage kid who didn't know any better, I

About 10 percent of the muzzleloading hunters in the country today hang on to their traditional ways, preferring to hunt with rifle designs and loads from the past.

took every deer I shot at with the rifle. And before moving up to a larger bore during the early 1970s, I managed to harvest about a dozen whitetails with the old percussion .45 caliber Dixie rifle, which I bought brand new in late summer of 1963 for just $79.50, plus $3.00 for shipping.

The muzzleloader that likely did more to popularize muzzleloader hunting than any other during the 1960s was the Hopkins & Allen under-hammer rifle. First offered in 1962 by Numrich Arms, of West Hurley, New York, the modern copies of the distinctly American under-hammer percussion ignition rifles were available in a choice of .36 or .45 caliber—offering a bore size for hunting either small or deer-sized game. The simple bottom-mounted hammer and direct into-the-powder nipple placement made these light, fast-handling little muzzleloading rifles the "In-Lines" of their day. The rifles were reliable, sure-fire and, for hunters on a tight budget, very economically priced. In fact, the plain "round barrel" model offered in 1962 could be bought for just $44.50, and the rifle came with a round ball mold, a flask with a quarter-pound of black powder, 100 percussion caps and a powder measure. Many muzzleloading hunters got their start with this muzzleloader.

Through the 1960s, the .45 caliber bore reigned in popularity. While not the best bore size for deer and other big game, it got the job done. At the same time, it was still very economical to shoot bore size for the target shooter, and was noted for its inherent accuracy. Companies like Replica Arms, Centennial Arms and a few other fledgling reproduction importers also came to market with new and improved muzzleloading rifles, the majority of which were offered in the very popular and versatile .45 caliber.

The .45 Begins to Lose Ground

At about the same time Dixie Gun Works was making the switch from .40 to .45 caliber with their Belgium-made longrifle, another new reproduction gun importer headed up by Val Forgett introduced a truly big-bore rifle for the muzzleloading hunter looking for added knockdown power. That gun was the .58 caliber Navy Arms Buffalo Hunter.

Navy Arms also had its start during the mid- to late 1950s, introducing in 1958 the first Italian-made reproduction of a .36 caliber Colt Model 1851 "Navy"

percussion six-gun. (That's how the company got its name.) A few years later, Val Forgett brought to Civil War buffs a modern copy of a big .58 caliber rifle, a reproduction of the colorful Remington "Zouave." Then, during the early 1960s, the company began to cater to the growing number of muzzleloading big game hunters by offering a sporterized half-stock version of the gun, which was dubbed the "Buffalo Hunter." The big percussion hunting rifle could be loaded with massive amounts of black powder behind either a patched .570 round ball (278 grains) or a big hollow-based conical "Minié" bullet that could top 500-grains. It was definitely a step up from the .45 caliber bores—a giant step up!

In 1962, a small gun-making operation known as Tingle Manufacturing also began to offer a well-made copy of the half-stock hunting rifles from the mid-1800s. While they were sold as the Model 1962 Target Rifle, the guns brought to American shooters the first modern-made .50 caliber muzzleloading big game rifle. The rifle also introduced muzzleloader shooters to double-set triggers and the use of a modern coil mainspring for smoother and more reliable operation of the lock. While those who made the switch to the .50 caliber bore immediately realized its superior knockdown power over the .45 caliber, the real love affair with the half-inch bore did not get its start for nearly another 10 years.

The .50 Caliber Takes Over

Not many of the rifles produced during the 1960s were built to be shot with anything other than the patched round ball. Even the .50 caliber Tingle half-stock was built with a bore rifled with a one turn-in-52 inches rate of twist that was simply too slow for good accuracy with an elongated lead bullet. So, when Warren Center first sat down to design the now famous Thompson/Center Arms Hawken rifle, he also set out to design a harder hitting conical big game hunting bullet right along with the new muzzleloader.

The best way to describe the T/C Hawken is to say that it is a modern, stylized version of the sturdy half-stock working rifles that became favored by that hardy breed of 1830s and 1840s adventurers known as the "mountain men." The rifle T/C introduced in 1970 weighed 8½ pounds instead of 10 or 11 pounds like the original guns. And instead of the usual .52 or .54 caliber bore favored by the shop operated by Samuel and Jacob Hawken in St. Louis, the "original" T/C Hawken sported the then still most popular .45 caliber bore.

Today's traditional rifle shooter has a great selection to choose from, like the very nicely styled "Hatfield Rifle" percussion rifle, shown here with a custom-built Jack Garner flintlock.

The rifle had been designed with a rate of rifling twist that was something of a compromise. True "bullet" rifles generally feature a rifling twist ranging from 1-in-20 to 1-in-38 inches. The new made Hawken came with a one turn-in-48 inches pitch of the rifling grooves. Warren Center had designed right along with it the new "Maxi-Ball" conical. However, the T/C Hawken was not marketed as a "bullet" rifle alone. The company promoted it as a dual purpose front-loader, capable of shooting accurately both the patched round ball and the Maxi-Ball with equal authority.

Most new T/C Hawken rifle owners generally found the bore to shoot one or the other well out of a particular rifle with a specific powder charge, but few shot either projectile equally well. One thing became clearly evident, and that was the added knockdown power of the heavier Maxi-Ball conical. With a 90-grain charge of FFg black powder, the 28-inch barreled Hawken would get a patched .440 ball out of the muzzle at around 1,980 f.p.s., with 1,106 f.p.e. The same powder charge behind the 240-grain Maxi-Ball was slower to get the bullet out of the muzzle, at 1,659 f.p.s., but the heavier elongated bullet generated 1,467 f.p.e. Downrange at 100 yards, the Maxi-Ball would hit a whitetail with right at 1,000 foot-pounds of remaining energy, while the energy of the round ball load would be down to around 350 f.p.e.

With the growing demands for a harder-hitting muzzle-loaded big game rifle, Thompson/Center Arms introduced the .50 caliber version of the Hawken in early 1972—and the bore size has never looked back since. By the mid-1970s, the .50 caliber T/C Hawken and the 370-grain Maxi-Ball had become the most wide-

ly used muzzle-loaded big game hunting combo in the country. With a 100-grain charge of FFg black powder, the rifle would push the heavy lead conical bullet from the muzzle at 1,418 f.p.s, generating 1,652 f.p.e. Out at 100 yards, the big bullet would smack a whitetail… bear…or elk with more than 1,200 foot-pounds of remaining knockdown power.

By the late 1970s, the .45 caliber bore had all but died. Less than 10 percent of all muzzleloading rifle models sold then were of that caliber. On the other hand, the sales of .50 caliber guns had skyrocketed. Thompson/Center Arms had introduced a more economical half-stock known as the "Renegade" in .50 and .54 caliber, Dixie Gun Works replaced its original Belgium-produced "Kentucky" .45 caliber rifle with a .50 caliber copy of a Tennessee Mountain Rifle, Lyman began offering several new rifles in .50 and .54 caliber, and Navy Arms entered the "Hawken" market with one of the truer copies of the original Hawken rifle in .50 and .54 caliber. The .45 was definitely on its way out. By 1980, only a small handful of reproduction guns were still offered in the caliber that had been number one through the 1960s.

The Rise and Fall of the .54

Since Turner Kirkland's first reproduction muzzleloading rifle during the mid-1950s, there has been and still remains a number of shooters who feel that the patched round ball is the only truly authentic muzzleloader projectile. Of course, many of these shooters base this on the fact that the conical hunting bullet was

FAR LEFT: This unique over/under .50 caliber rifle was imported from Italy by Ive Johnson during the early 1980s. Loaded with Buffalo Bullet Company conicals, it shot well.

CENTER: Shown here are two of the author's early muzzle-loaded hunting rifles, which he built himself. The back rifle is a copy of a big .54 caliber "Hawken" half-stock. The scoped rifle is a hybrid traditional rifle with old-fashioned looks and a fast-twist barrel.

LEFT: Introduced by Ithaca Gun Company, this excellent copy of an original "Hawken" rifle is still available through Navy Arms as the Navy-Ithaca Hawken. It is offered in .50 and .54 caliber.

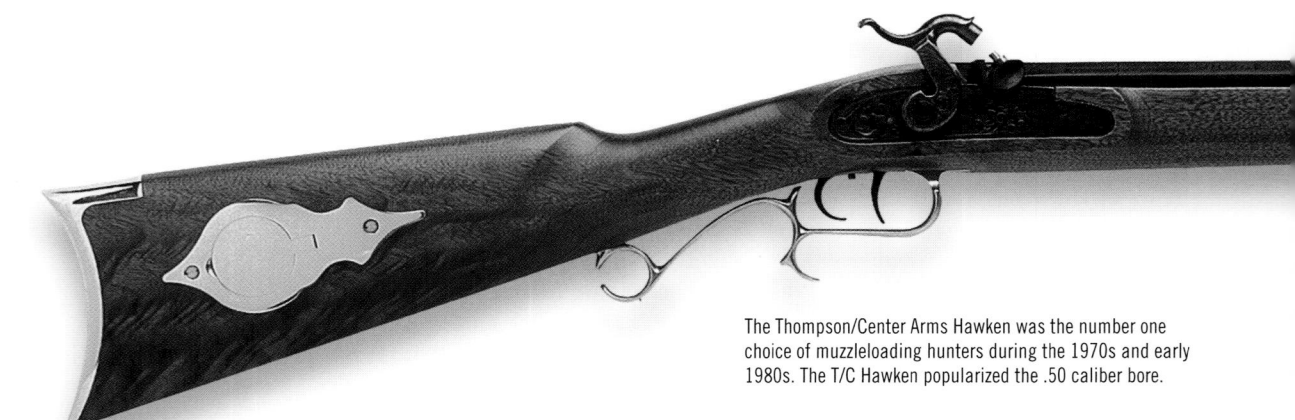

The Thompson/Center Arms Hawken was the number one choice of muzzleloading hunters during the 1970s and early 1980s. The T/C Hawken popularized the .50 caliber bore.

not fully developed until the 1830s and 1840s, post-dating the flintlock ignition system many of these same shooters work so hard to master.

Still, in order to deliver a more lethal blow to the larger game being hunted, these same shooters moved to the larger .50 and even larger .54 caliber bore sizes.

A Speer .440" swaged round ball weighs 128 grains, a .490" ball tips the scales at 177 grains and a .530" ball weighs in at 224 grains. With equal 90-grain charges of FFg black powder or Pyrodex RS/Select, each of these ball sizes shot from a 28-inch barrel of appropriate caliber will produce a slower velocity as a heavier ball is used. However, due to the added weight of the round ball for a larger caliber, the amount of energy produced increases dramatically. For instance, a .490 ball pushed from the muzzle of a .50 caliber rifle by 90 grains of FFg black powder is good for 1,950 f.p.s. with 1,478 f.p.e. When the same powder charge is loaded behind a .530 ball, it will get the heavier ball out of a .54 caliber bore at just 1,761 f.p.s., but generates 1,584 f.p.e. In other words, the slower-moving 224-grain ball produces 116 foot-pounds more energy than the lighter, but faster, 177-grain ball for the .50 caliber.

Another advantage of the slightly larger .54 caliber round-ball bore is that is offers greater burning capacity. Or, it will more efficiently consume heavier powder charges. While a 90-grain charge of FFg could prove to be the maximum efficient charge that can be shot out of a 28-inch .50 caliber round-ball barrel, the same barrel length with a larger .54 caliber hole running through the center may effectively consume an additional 10 to 20 grains. And if a 100-grain charge of FFg is shot behind a patched .530 ball in a 28-inch .54 caliber barrel, the load will give 1,855 f.p.s. at the muzzle, with 1,758 f.p.e. When shooting a patched round ball, the larger bore size will deliver greater game-taking performance.

While the rifle used by this hunter to take this buck may be of "traditional" design, no original side-hammer muzzleloaders were ever built with stainless steel or a synthetic stock.

Toward the end of the 1970s, round-ball rifles of .54 caliber accounted for as much as 35 percent of all traditional muzzleloader sales. However, when it came to performance on game, the .50 caliber rifles loaded with a modern conical bullet, such as the T/C Maxi-Ball or the Lee Precision REAL (Rifling Engraved At Loading) bullet would not only deliver greater knockdown power than a larger .54 loaded with a heavy powder charge and patched round ball, the magnum conical loads in the smaller bore rifle also tended to shoot flatter and more accurately at longer range. The heavier conical bullets also created more compression on the burning powder charge, again allowing better consumption of heavier charges. A 100-grain charge of Pyrodex RS behind a 250-grain Lee REAL Bullet would produce right at 1,650 f.p.s. at the muzzle of a 28-inch .50 caliber barrel, giving the hunter just over 1,500 foot-pounds of muzzle energy. Due to the better aerodynamics of the lighter conical bullet, the load would actually hit a deer at 100 yards with around 1,100 f.p.e., or around 400 more foot-pounds of knockdown power than a .530 ball that may have generated several hundred foot-pounds of additional energy at the muzzle.

With the introduction of the modern in-line rifles during the mid- to late 1980s, and the switch to shooting modern plastic saboted bullets, the .54 caliber rifles really began to lose in popularity. By then, muzzleloading had become a true hunting sport, and optimum performance had become the name of the game. Shooters had discovered that the .50 could and would do just about anything the .54 caliber bores could do—and generally do it more cost effectively, more accurately and with less recoil. Today, the .54 caliber rifles account for only about 5 percent of all muzzleloaders sold.

While muzzleloader shooting has appealed to all genders, all ages and people from all walks of life, many of those who prefer the traditionally styled guns do not hunt.

Great Traditional Rifle Choices Available

If you still have the desire to shoot and hunt with a rifle of very authentic design, there are plenty of great choices presently available. In fact, many of the "reproduction" muzzleloading rifles now offered are some of the more authentically styled guns to ever be offered. The current selection still includes the Thompson/Center Arms Hawken, the Dixie Gun Works Tennessee Mountain Rifle, the Lyman Great Plains Rifle, a copy of the Harper's Ferry 1803 flintlock rifle from Navy Arms, .45 and .50 caliber Kentucky reproductions from companies like Traditions and Cabela's, while the Italian maker Pedersoli offers a wide range of outstanding copies of early to mid-1800s muzzleloading guns through a number of major U.S. importers. Austin & Halleck even offers a beautiful rendition of a nicely styled .50 caliber Rocky Mountain rifle that's offered in flint or percussion ignition, with the choice of 1-in-66 inches rate of twist for shooting the patched round ball, or a 1-in-28 inches rate of twist for shooting modern conical or saboted bullets.

Today, there is most definitely a muzzleloading rifle model available to satisfy any taste or need, whether it's traditional, modern or something in between.

Custom muzzleloading rifle maker Jack Garner prepares to shoot one of his fine authentic re-creations as a curious onlooker watches as he primes the pan of the flintlock ignition system.

modern bore-sized
CONICAL HUNTING BULLETS

For the most part, elongated conical bullets for muzzleloading rifles were developed between about 1830 and 1860. Most early attempts were for military purposes in order to provide a muzzle-loaded projectile that could be rammed down the bore more quickly and easily than a patched round ball. Military tactics of the time still relied on "volume of fire" rather than "precise shot placement," and the outcome of a battle very often swung in favor of the side that had managed to get off the highest number of volleys.

The most successful of these early bullets were the variations of the big, hollow-based Minié bullet that was used extensively during the Civil War. Named after the French captain who designed it, the Minié was indeed designed more for easy loading, and reloading, than for pinpoint long-range accuracy. These great hunks of pure lead generally featured a rounded nose, several "grease grooves" that encircled the base of the bullet, and a deep hollow base. One of the .575 diameter bullets could practically be dropped right into the clean bore of a .58 caliber (.580 bore) rifled-musket and seated over the powder charge by the weight of the ramrod which would practically push the bullet down over the powder.

Surprisingly, some of the better quality rifled-muskets of the era were extremely accurate with such a loose fitting bullet. The Minié was simple in design, and effective. The undersized projectile loaded extremely easy, and when the powder charge was ignited behind it, the pressures created caused the hollow base to expand into the rifling, sealing off the bore. If the original Minié bullet design had one flaw, it was probably the thin and fragile "skirt" at the rear of the bullet. The standard service load of the Civil War was around 60 grains of FFg black powder. If a much heavier charge was used, the added pressure would tend to blow through the thin lead skirt created by the hollow base propelling the round but leaving a ring of lead stuck in the barrel.

The military minds of the mid-1850s weren't the only ones to realize the benefits of an elongated muzzle-loaded projectile. Hunters, too, realized the potential of something other than a patched round ball. However, instead of faster, easier loading, most realized that a longer, heavier bullet would offer greater knockdown power, better downrange retention of that energy, and with rifling having the proper "twist" or "pitch," such bullets could prove to be extremely accurate. In other words, many of the hunters from the mid-1850s were looking for the same thing most of us today continually seek—better performance on big game.

FAR LEFT: Game as large as elk require proper shot placement and enough energy to deliver a lethal blow. Big, heavy conical bullets, weighing 350 to 500 grains can deliver that kind of performance, especially when hunting in close cover.

Before the refinement of the elongated hunting bullet during the 1840s, hunters looking for added knockdown power simply shot larger bore rifles, like the custom copy of a Hawken shown here, with massive powder charges behind a large diameter round ball. (The rifle here was built by the author.)

Probably the earliest known improvement over the round ball by American rifle makers and shooters appeared around 1835. These bullets were known as "sugarloaf" or "picket" bullets. The base of this design was still rounded, much like the curved surface of a round ball, and there was little, if any, true cylindrical shape to the body of the bullet, since many of these had been designed to still be loaded with a patch. Some featured a flat front nose, others a somewhat rounded point. The latter were also known as "acorn" bullets, since they resembled an acorn.

Loading such designs often proved difficult. Without a true cylindrical body, shooters found it hard to keep the nose of the bullet perfectly centered in the bore and a bullet that was slightly canted one way or the other would fly erratically once it left the bore. Within a few years, improved designs with cylindrical shape were introduced, and muzzleloading hunters around the world quickly abandoned the round ball in favor of harder-hitting and longer-range bullet rifles.

Possibly the most impressive bullet and rifle designs dating from the 1850s were the product of an Englishman named Sir Joseph Whitworth. In 1854, he was granted a patent for his hexagonal muzzle-loaded bore and mechanically fitted elongated bullet. In official tests by the British War Office, Whitworth's rifle and bullet outperformed—accuracy wise—any other muzzle-loaded firearm ever officially tested. His .450 caliber rifle would consistently keep his 530-grain 1.32-inch-long-paper patched and mechanically started bullet inside of 4 inches at 500 yards. Whitworth's system was not adopted by the British Service for two reasons: the oddity of the hexagonal bore (and the difficulties of producing the barrel), and the slow loading of the mechanically fitted bullet. Instead, the War Office went with the .577 Enfield rifled-musket and the easy to load Minié bullet. However, a few Whitworth rifles did see service during the Civil War as long-range sniper rifles, often fitted with an early, long brass-tube scope.

As the new breech-loading cartridge rifles quickly replaced muzzle-loaded guns after the Civil War, further development of muzzleloader projectiles slowed greatly. Only a small group of target shooters continued to use muzzleloading rifles. Even so, through the last half of the 1800s and into the early 1900s, some of the rifles and bullets designed by serious shooters of the period produced accuracy that, to this day, has not been matched by any muzzleloader since. One group the author was privileged to see was 10-shots at 200 yards that had a maximum outside spread of just 1.7 inches. It was shot by noted target rifle maker and shooter A. O. "Pop" Niedner in 1939 with a .40 caliber under-hammer bullet rifle of his own make, shooting a paper patched and mechanically started elongated bullet that was three times the caliber in length.

Conical Bullets
for the Modern-Day Hunter

Today's muzzleloading hunter is just as concerned with getting as much punch and retained downrange energy as any hunter from the past. While the majority of those who head out with a muzzle-loaded rifle thrown over their shoulder in pursuit of deer and other big game now rely on modern plastic saboted bullets (see Chapter 6), there remains a substantial number of very serious big game hunters who still prefer shooting and hunting with the bore-sized conical lead bullets. When time is taken to work up a load for a rifle that will shoot them accurately, there is no denying that these great hunks of lead are extremely effective on big game.

An added benefit of most commercially produced conical designs now available is that the bullets also load a lot easier than any other type of muzzle-loaded projectile. Lead has no memory, meaning that once the rifling has cut into any oversized band or bullet surface, that bullet can then be easily pushed down the bore with a minimum amount of pressure on the ramrod. Shooters who have found tight fitting sabot and bullet combinations next to impossible to push down the bore of their rifle very often switch to one of the easy loading conical designs, without giving up much in the way of performance.

At one time, knowledgeable muzzleloading shooters generally only considered two factors when looking to match a conical bullet to a particular rifle: the caliber of the rifle and the rate of rifling twist in the bore. However, this was during the days when muzzleloading shooters really only had one suitable propellant, and that was black powder. Velocity of the load then only played a very minor role in determining which bullet to load and shoot.

While the original era of the elongated muzzleloading bullet was a relatively short one, lasting roughly 30 to 40 years, quite a bit of thought went into the designs that prevailed—and into the rifles that shot these bullets accurately. As early as 1830, scientists and engineers had started tabulating

A somewhat younger and more whiskered Toby Bridges with a trophy class Wyoming pronghorn taken with his custom .50 caliber "bullet rifle" and 385-grain Buffalo Bullet Company conical bullet at around 220 yards.

formulas for precisely determining the rates of rifling twist for best accuracy with conical bullets. One of the most widely used was based on the "Greenhill Formula," which established the necessary pitch of rifling for accuracy with a cannon. A few years later, another Englishman named Major J. P. Cundill used the same formula to establish the proper twist for muzzle-loaded rifle projectiles.

The formula was based on the length of the projectile, giving the necessary rate of twist for proper stabilization of the bullet in calibers instead of inches. For instance, if a bullet is twice as long (two calibers) as it is in diameter (actual caliber), then the required rate of rifling twist would be one turn-in-84.29 calibers. Let's take an easier to understand look at the conversions Cundill established. If a .45 caliber bullet is .900 in length, or two calibers long, the required rate of twist for proper stabilization (and accuracy) would be rifling with a turn-in-37.93 inches, or to round it off one turn-in-38 inches. For a really long bullet like Whitworth's 1.32-inch-long 530-grain bullet (3 calibers in length), Cundill's table called for rifling with one turn-in-50.74 calibers. Or, rifling that spun with a full turn-in-22.83 inches. Rifle makers of the period followed these tables fairly closely, generally producing molds for bullets of the right length to match the pitch of the rifling.

The White in-line rifles have been designed and built specifically for shooting long, heavy bore-sized conical bullets.

When Thompson/Center Arms introduced their "Hawken" rifle back in 1971, right along with it they introduced a new conical bullet design known as the T/C "Maxi-Ball." The company went with a one turn-in-48 inches rate of rifling twist for both the .45 and .50 caliber bores they offered during the early 1970s. The rifle was marketed as a dual purpose "patched round ball" and "bullet" rifle. However, most Hawken owners discovered that their individual rifle would usually shoot one or the other of the projectile types accurately, but not both. The 370-grain .50 caliber T/C Maxi measures right at .88, or in other words the bullet is basically 1.75 times longer than it is in diameter. Using the Cundill formula, we come up with a turn-in-46 inches as the right twist—give an inch or two—for this particular bullet. According to the 150-year-old formula, T/C was pretty darn close with their turn-in-48 inches rate of twist.

Let's take a look at a few other popular heavylead bore-sized conical bullets currently available, and what the Cundill "Table of Twists for Small Arms Projectiles" says should be the ideal rate of rifling twist for those bullets.

The Buffalo Bullet Company 385-grain .50 caliber conical measures .820" in length, or 1.64 times its diameter. The rate of twist that should shoot this bullet best would be somewhere around a turn-in-46 inches. The 440-grain Parker Hydra-Con bore-sized .50 caliber bullet measures .930" in length, or 1.86 calibers. The rate of twist for this one would be 1-in-44 inches. The .50 caliber 500-grain Parker Hydra-Con measures 1.1" in length, or 2.2 times its diameter. Again, according to the Cundill tables, the right rate of twist for this one would be a turn-in-38 inches. The White 460-grain .450 PowerPunch bullet measures a lengthy 1.2", or 2.7 times its caliber. The rate of twist for this one would be around a turn-in-25 inches.

Back when the Cundill rate of twist tables were formulated, not many shooters were loading with charges as heavy as 100 grains of black powder. Today, just about any shooter looking to tap the full performance of a heavy lead conical bullet will stoke that rifle with 100…120…130…or more grains of powder in order to get that big bullet out of the muzzle at a decent velocity. And velocity has become a very important third factor when determining the best rate of rifling twist for a particular length of bullet in a given bore size. It is a rare rifle indeed that will give equal, or even near equal, accuracy with both a long, heavy bullet and a much lighter and shorter bullet. If there is a conical bullet rifle in your future, you will either be faced with first determining the length and weight of bullet you intend to shoot, then finding a rifle with the proper rate of twist—or, pick out the rifle you like and find the length and weight of bullet it shoots best. The latter is the route most shooters take, since it's a lot cheaper to buy new bullets than a new rifle.

Today's Top-Quality Conical Bullets

Despite all the performance claims by the different manufacturers of bore-sized lead conical bullets, there really isn't a whole lot of difference in the design or terminal performance from one bullet to another—with an exception or two. Soft, pure lead is pretty well soft, pure lead and the vast majority of bullets, while maybe of slightly different outside contour, basically rely on one or more slightly over-sized bearing bands, rings or surfaces that must be lightly engraved by the rifling during loading. When it comes down to accuracy, it is usually the consistent uniformity of a particular brand of conical bullet that makes it shoot better than another.

Just how much energy a conical bullet produces is entirely reliant upon the weight of the bullet and the velocity a shooter is able to get it out of the muzzle. As for heavier bore-sized bullets having more drop than a lighter bullet of similar design, keep in mind that all projectiles, whether they weigh 100 grains or 500 grains, drop about 16 feet in the first second of flight. The law of gravity is what actually determines drop. However, a lighter bullet with a higher muzzle velocity will get to the target faster than a heavier, slower moving conical bullet. And due to the faster flight time to 100 or 200 yards, the lighter bullet will appear to have less drop.

This .45 caliber White Power Punch bore-sized bullet weighs a whopping 460 grains. With a 100-grain charge of black powder, Pyrodex or Triple Seven, it would deliver quite a punch on game as large as moose.

Toby Bridges built this custom muzzleloading big game rifle specifically to shoot big conical bullets like the hollow-point Buffalo Bullet Company bullets in this photo. The rifle was built with a fast-twist bore.

For the most part, .54 conical bullet rifles have pretty well come and gone. Shooters have discovered that they can generate the same energy levels, with accuracy, with a .50 caliber rifle loaded with a 400-grain bullet as they could a .54 loaded with the same weight bullet and powder charge. And, for the most part, it is easier to get the desired accuracy with the slightly smaller bore. The same holds true when going down to the .45 from a .50. Not many knowledgeable conical bullet shooters will choose a .50 or .54 over the .45 caliber when it comes to accuracy. Some of the most accurate front-loading rifles ever built were .45s with a fast-twist bore for shooting long, heavy lead conical bullets. Unfortunately, a few states will not allow muzzleloading rifles of that caliber to be used on really big game, like elk, even though with a big bullet like the .450 White 380- or 430-grain PowerPunch Bullets and 90 to 120 grains of FFg black powder or Pyrodex "RS/Select," a .45 bullet rifle will definitely outperform most .50 caliber rifles loaded with a bullet of similar weight and the same powder charge.

Commercially produced conical bullets for .45, .50 and .54 caliber high per-

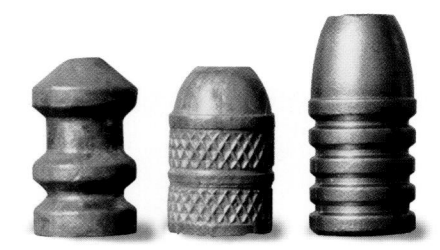

Shown here are three commonly used bore-sized conical bullets, left to right: T/C 370-grain .50 caliber Maxi-Ball; Buffalo Bullet Company 385-grain hollow-pointed .50 caliber bullet; and the 480-grain Parker Hydra-Con conical for .50 caliber rifles.

The "Power Belt" bullet is a modern approach to shooting an old projectile design, by adding a plastic "skirt" or "gas seal" to the rear of the bullet. Shown here is the 195-grain "Power Belt" bullet for the .45 caliber bore.

formance muzzleloading big game rifles are now available from a dozen or more suppliers, plus there are quality molds available that increase the selection even more for the shooter willing to cast his own. Just out of a .50 caliber bore, today's shooter can choose from bullets weighing anywhere from 250 to more than 500 grains. (Parker Productions, of Spring Creek, Nevada offers one .50 caliber behemoth that tops 700 grains!) The selection for the .45 caliber rifles is nearly as impressive, with bullets from around 200 grains up to nearly 500 grains.

One of the more unique conical designs currently available is the Power Belt Bullet (originally sold as the "Black Belt") produced by the Power Belt Bullet Company. What sets this bullet apart from other conical bullets currently available is that this design features a plastic skirt attached to the rear of the bullet. Many shooters mistakenly think that this is there to provide a gas seal. Wrong, the main purpose of the slightly oversized skirt, which snaps onto a short post protruding from the rear center of the bullet, is to hold the undersized bullet in place over the powder charge. Upon ignition, obturation (flattening of the bullet) causes the bullet to squat slightly in the bore, filling the shallow grooves of a true bullet bore and forming the necessary gas seal. And it is a combination of exceptional accuracy and easy loading that has made the Power Belt Bullet one of today's most popular conical designs.

Years ago, before the introduction of the Knight in-line rifles and saboted bullets, I spent most of one summer building my own .50 caliber bullet rifle. I used the reliable percussion lock and double-set triggers from a Thompson/Center

Hawken rifle and a beautiful curly maple stock from the old stock maker Reinhart Fajen (then of Warsaw, Missouri). While I did shoot some with a factory .50 caliber T/C barrel, I knew I needed a faster twist to get the kind of accuracy I was looking for from a conical bullet. I convinced the old H&H Barrel Works to turn me one of their .50 caliber barrels (.503 land to land) with a stepped-up one turn-in-24 inches rate of rifling twist.

For the bullet, I went to a machinist friend who cut a .50 caliber mold for a long conical bullet in a modified Whitworth design with four fairly deep grease grooves, weighing 485 grains. The bullets measured .508 across, and before loading were forced through a swaging die. Bullets that had been run through the die consistently measured .506 at the bands between the grease grooves and at the base and nose bands. It took a relatively healthy whack on a short starter that precisely fit the nose of the bullet to engrave the soft lead bands with the rifling. But once the bullet was in the bore, it could be easily pushed down with the ramrod.

Muzzleloading hunter Garth Carter prepares to field dress more than 1,400 pounds of Alaskan moose he dropped with a single 400-grain White .45 caliber soft lead conical bullet.

I installed one of the long eye-relief 4x Redfield handgun scopes well forward of the ignition system, and with a 120-grain charge of FFg black powder, I found the rifle capable of printing honest 1½-inch, 100-yard groups. Several times, I shot the rifle at 200 yards and found that it was capable of keeping shots inside of 4 inches. The longest shot I ever made with the rig was at 219 yards at a 15-inch horned pronghorn buck. The big bullet literally bowled over the 125-pound antelope.

When working up the load for this rifle, at first I could not get the accuracy I had hoped for. On some days, 4 to 5 inches at a hundred was the best I could hope for. And too often, I'd experience a wild flier that impacted on the target paper a good 7 or 8 inches from the other shots. Then I did a little research on the loading techniques of the "old-time" bullet rifle shooters of the late 1800s and learned how they would very often load a heavy waxed card wad...a lubricated felt wool wad...or both between the bullet and the powder charge to reduce the erosion and deformation of the bullet base. And by doing just that—using a heavy .125 waxed card wad directly over the powder, followed by a .50 caliber lubed wool wad—my accuracy problems were cured. Recently, I have replaced the waxed card and felt wads with the obturator cup (gas seal) cut from the base of a Winchester 28-gauge "AA" wad. This old rifle now shoots better than ever.

If the plastic saboted bullets now used by the majority of today's performance-minded hunters do not appeal to you, whether because of loading difficulties or just the thought of taking muzzleloading to that degree of modern technology but you still want far better performance than possible with the patched round ball, there's a modern conical bullet rifle and bullet out there that's ideal for you. White Rifles (Orem, Utah) markets a super selection of modern in-line ignition rifles that have been designed for use with the company's excellent line of conical lead bullets. The rifles are offered in .451 (1-20 inch twist) and .504 (1-24 inch twist) caliber. However, if you're looking for a rifle of more traditional design, but want the knockdown power of a heavy lead conical bullet, the 32-inch barreled Austin & Halleck (Provo, Utah) .50 caliber Mountain Rifle with its one turn-in-28 inches twist rifling should fill the bill nicely.

the in-line
IGNITION REVOLUTION

For muzzleloading, the age of innocence has now come and gone. When it comes to "sure-fire" ignition, the days of "Gosh…By Golly…It went off!" are now long behind us. In fact, many of today's more efficient in-line ignition muzzle-loaded big game rifles are so reliable, the modern-day hunter who follows the rifle manufacturer's loading instructions can literally expect 100 percent ignition every time the hammer falls on a capped nipple or, with many of today's advanced in-line rifle models, a primed chamber. And when loaded with the latest black powder substitute and saboted bullet, many of these not-so-old-fashioned front-loading rifles will actually shoot just as hard and accurately as many popular center-fire hunting rifles.

FAR LEFT: Modern in-line ignition rifles changed muzzle-loading forever, bringing not only ultra modern looks, but very modern performance to the sport.

Thumb through practically any current shooting and hunting publication and you're sure to find advertisements for the newest muzzleloading guns with headlines and sales copy making boasts like, "Muzzle energy equivalent to a 7mm Remington Mag," "Hard hitting accuracy beyond 100 yards," or "The Most Powerful .50 cal. Muzzleloader in the World!" It quickly becomes pretty clear that muzzleloading has become a performance-driven sport. And there is now a new breed of muzzleloading hunter out there who continues to demand greater accuracy and knockdown power. Until now, such performance from a muzzle-loaded big game rifle had been impossible to obtain.

In-Line Rifles Come of Age

The front-loaded hunting rifle that can be credited with starting the in-line craze was the Knight MK-85. It didn't take serious muzzleloading hunters long to realize that by placing the nipple directly in the rear center of the breech plug, the Knight design not only made ignition more positive, it also made ignition more reliable. Fire from an exploding percussion cap had to travel just a fraction of an inch to reach the powder charge in the barrel, ensuring fast and sure-fire ignition. Within five years after this ignition system hit the market, hunters began making a mass exodus from older and less reliable side-hammer designs.

Contrary to popular belief, William "Tony" Knight did not invent the in-line percussion ignition system. There are a number of surviving originals to establish that the concept was around during the early 1800s, plus there were several other modern in-line ignition rifles around that predate the introduction of

Knight's first MK-85 in 1985.

One of the earliest modern day in-line ignition rifles to be sold was the Esopus Pacer, a sleek in-line percussion rifle that was on the market during the early 1970s. This 26-inch barreled muzzleloader was built with some very modern features—even by today's standards. The rifle was built with an in-line ignition system that automatically put the safety in the "on" position anytime the side-mounted hammer was cocked. And for convenience, the safety was located on the forward curve of the trigger guard. To move the safety into the "off" position only required the shooter to push forward on the guard-mounted safety with his trigger finger.

When this rifle was introduced in 1972, it was available only in .45 caliber. However, at that time, the .45 bore was the most popular among the growing ranks of muzzleloading shooters. The vast majority of muzzleloader hunting seasons were still well into the future. Unfortunately, the Esopus Pacer was too advanced for the time it was introduced. Keep in mind, shooters during the early 1970s were turning to muzzleloading primarily to experience shooting, and to a smaller degree hunting, with a front-loaded design from the past. The Pacer was just too modern looking for the period, and saw very limited production and sales.

About 10 years later, another very modern-looking rifle of in-line ignition again hit the market, the Michigan Arms Wolverine. This rifle, offered in .50 and .54 caliber and built with hot No. 209 primer ignition, easily could have realized the success enjoyed by the Knight in-line rifle if the manufacturer had built the guns with a barrel designed for something other than the patched round ball. During the early 1980s, muzzleloader hunting for big game had taken hold, and hunters were already looking for all the knockdown power they could get from a muzzle-loaded big game rifle.

Although the Michigan Arms Wolverine predated the Knight MK-85 by

William "Tony" Knight, shown here with a good pronghorn taken with a later model Knight rifle, can be credited with bringing to the market the first in-line rifle model with the features that appealed to the modern-day hunter.

three or four years, the slow one turn-in-66 inches rate of rifling twist found in the barrel of the earlier in-line pretty well proved to be the death blow for the muzzleloader. A rate of twist this slow is good for shooting just one type of projectile—the patched round ball. Hunters across the country were already making the switch to a number of much harder-hitting heavy lead conical bullets that definitely did a better job of putting big game down. Muzzleloader hunting was entering a new era, in which optimum accuracy and big game stopping power suddenly took precedence over a muzzleloader of traditional styling. The round ball simply didn't cut it as a hunting projectile any longer.

Knight MK-85 Development

The Knight MK-85 brought to the muzzleloading market the first modern in-line ignition muzzleloading hunting rifle built with all of the features serious muzzleloading big game hunters wanted, plus a few many had never even thought

of before. In addition to its fast, efficient in-line percussion ignition, the MK-85 featured great handling in a compact modern rifle design. It also allowed easy scope mounting, thanks to a receiver that came predrilled and tapped, plus this rifle was also equipped with two safeties and a removable breech plug that made the rifle the easiest to clean muzzleloader ever offered. Still, even with all of these great features, the MK-85 was not an overnight success. The great performance this muzzle-loaded rifle became known for required a few more years of refinement to the rifle, plus more work with the then brand-new saboted bullet system.

ABOVE: The Knight double safety system is actually the only feature that was patented on these early models.

RIGHT: Hunters familiar with modern firearms immediately took to the Knight MK-85 since the rifle was built with the looks, feel and many of the features found on their center-fire big game rifles.

Back in February 1986, Tony Knight sent me one of his very first in-line rifles to shoot and evaluate. The serial number on that rifle was number 31. The .50 caliber rifle received was just about everything the modern-day muzzleloading hunter could hope for—with super efficient ignition, a positive safety system, great balance, removable breech plug for easy and thorough cleaning, and more. That rifle shot the then still new conical bullets from Buffalo Bullet Company better than anything else this writer had shot them out of. The very first MK-85 rifles featured a one turn-in-48 inches rate of rifling twist that did an admirable job with many of the new bore-sized conical lead bullets on the market at that time. However, the rate of twist was still too slow for turning in acceptable accuracy with the brand-new projectile system that featured a jacketed hand-gun bullet gripped by the sleeves of a small plastic "wad" called a sabot.

Fortunately, in 1987 Knight made the switch to a faster 1:32 inches rate of twist and the still new company's MK-85 began shooting the saboted bullets with greater accuracy. However, this system did not begin to realize its full performance potential until the twist was stepped up to 1:28 inches just a couple of years later. That is the same rate of twist found in most Knight Rifles barrels since. And it has been that rate of twist with saboted bullets that became the standard that most of the following in-line ignition rifle models were either originally built with or quickly adopted. It has proven to be a nearly unbeatable combination with a wide range of bullet weights and bullet lengths.

Knight's earlier turn-in-32 inches rate of twist generally performed well with shorter 240- to 260-grain saboted .451- or .452-inch diameter bullets, but when loaded with a bullet that was considerably longer, accuracy was less than ideal. Ten years after the Knight 1:32 barrels were replaced by faster 1:28 twist barrels, owners of the older .50 caliber models with the slower twist usually found that the rifling would not stabilize the exceptionally long all-copper 300-grain Barnes Expander MZ bullets. Not only was accuracy poor, but the bullets would regularly keyhole badly and print on target paper sideways!

While not the first modern in-line percussion ignition hunting rifle on the market, the Knight MK-85 was the first rifle of its type to deliver the stepped-up performance demanded by today's muzzleloading hunter. Tony Knight definitely paved the way for the dozens of other in-line ignition rifles that have followed.

In-Line Rifle Evolution

The metamorphosis of the high performance muzzleloading big game rifle remained in high gear through the 1990s, and continues today. Knight Rifles, Thompson/Center Arms, White Rifles, Gonic Arms, Traditions, Connecticut Valley Arms and a few other muzzleloader manufacturers have continually accelerated the evolution of the in-line ignition front-loader. The competition for the dollars muzzleloading hunters have to spend has been good for this industry, resulting in newer, more efficient designs that almost make the simple plunger hammer design of Knight's original MK-85 and similarly designed rifles seem somewhat old fashioned.

Improved manufacturing techniques and more thought-out designs now allow in-line rifle makers to actually produce a better performing big game rifle at a more affordable price. As the 1990s wound down, a muzzleloading hunter could purchase a more advanced in-line rifle for $250 to $300 that would actually out-

The Knight in-line rifles were the first to feature a removable breech plug, which made cleaning much faster and easier.

When Modern Muzzleloading, Inc. made the switch to a faster rifling twist to tap the performance of the new saboted projectile system, the popularity of the rifles and new bullet system both began to skyrocket. (The 260-grain Speer .451" jacketed hollow-point is shown here.)

perform late 1980s model in-lines that may have carried $400 to $500 price tags. By the beginning of the new millennium, the popularity of these rifles had soared to the point where sales of the in-lines easily accounted for 80 percent (or more) of the entire muzzleloader market. In one year alone, Knight Rifles built and shipped more than 100,000 in-line ignition rifles, 90+ percent of them in the popular .50 caliber.

Remington Arms Company took in-line ignition muzzleloading design to a new level in 1996 with the introduction of their revered Model 700 bolt-action center-fire line in an all-new muzzle-loaded configuration. Built around a modified Model 700 receiver and bolt, the Model 700ML gave shooters and hunters a front-loading rifle with a considerably faster hammer fall than possible with any of the plunger-hammer style in-line ignition systems. However, when it came to actual ballistics, the Remington Model 700ML, and other similarly styled "bolt-action" in-line rifles that followed, did not shoot any faster, flatter or harder than any conventional plunger-hammer in-line design. However, shooters seemed to like the quicker lock time of a true bolt, and within a year or two of the Model 700ML introduction, Ruger entered the market with their bolt-action Model 77/50…Connecticut Valley Arms introduced their Firebolt model…Traditions brought out their now popular Lightning model…and a new firm known as Austin & Halleck hit the market with an extremely classy looking bolt-action in-line percussion rifle. Some of these rifles were offered in several different calibers, but it was the .50 caliber that continued to reign in popularity.

Knight has continued to be a leader in in-line rifle development, with most current models based on the *Disc Ignition System Concept* that was introduced during the mid- to late 1990s.

Knight Rifles was not to be outdone by this latest round of muzzleloader development, introducing in 1997 the D.I.S.C. Rifle. The model designation stands for "Disc Ignition System Concept," an idea that once again took modern muzzleloader development to yet another, higher level. The original D.I.S.C. Rifle design was a unique bolt-action design that eliminated the use of a nipple in the ignition system, and instead of the standard No. 11 percussion cap, this Tony Knight design relied on a much hotter No. 209 shot-shell primer for putting more fire into the barrel for still better ignition of the powder charge.

The design incorporates a small plastic disc that becomes the carrier for the No. 209 primer. This disc is then somewhat compressed between the face of the bolt and the rear of the breech plug. While some of the fire from the primer is lost between the fit of the plastic disc and the breech plug, the system still puts considerably more fire into the barrel than possible with a nipple and No. 11 cap. (Knight now offers a newer D.I.S.C. Extreme model that fully encloses the plastic carrier for the primer, eliminating much of the fire loss.)

Not only does the hotter flame of a No. 209 primer mean more reliable ignition, it also results in better consumption of heavier magnum powder charges. Knight became one of the first companies to promote the use of three 50-grain Pyrodex Pellet loads (150-grain charge) for increased velocity and greater knockdown power for big game. Thompson/Center Arms also quickly jumped on the magnum muzzleloader bandwagon with the introduction of their Encore 209x50 Magnum muzzleloader shortly after Knight's debut of the D.I.S.C. Rifle. However, instead of a bolt-action design, Thompson/Center elected to build their front-loading .50 caliber powerhouse on the break-open action of their popular single-shot cartridge handgun (and later rifle) also produced under the Encore name. The one thing the new T/C rifle shared with the Knight bolt-action was that it, too, relied on hotter No. 209 primers for ignition—and for a more complete burn of three 50-grain Pyrodex Pellets.

Today, just about every in-line muzzleloading rifle maker is promoting the use of 150-grain pellet charges—either Pyrodex or the newer Triple Seven powder. (Both are from Hodgdon Powder Company.) Oddly enough, a few of the importers to join the race to offer the fastest-shooting and hardest-hitting muzzleloaded big game rifle once stated in their owner's manuals that powder charges of 100 to 120 grains should be considered absolute maximum loads for these rifles. The guns they sell today still use the same steel, and other than the modification to allow the use of shotgun primers for ignition, the designs of their ignition systems have changed little. Even the proof test stamping on the barrels remains the same. All that seems to have changed has been their performance claims.

These days, no one wants to have the slowest shooting in-line rifle that produces the lowest amount of game-taking energy. Consequently, a few of these companies are now making some pretty outlandish claims about the velocities and energy levels produced by their rifles when loaded with magnum powder charges and saboted bullets. One very knowledgeable shooter I know, who has done extensive ballistics work with many of the same rifles and loads, pretty well summed up much of the sales hype as "voodoo ballistics!" And, after putting thousands of muzzle-loaded rounds across the screens of a chronograph myself, I have to agree with him.

In-Line Ballistics

One of my favorite loads for an early Knight MK-85 (late 1980s production) was 100 grains of Pyrodex "RS/Select" behind a Muzzleload Magnum Products standard black sabot with a 250-grain .452" Hornady XTP jacketed hollow-point bullet. At the muzzle of the 24-inch barrel, the load would consistently give me right at 1,620 f.p.s. This translates into 1,455 f.p.e. That rifle and load easily accounted for nearly 50 deer-sized big-game animals during the four or five years I hunted with it, taken with shots from 30 to 150 yards, and not one ever required a second shot.

Today, close to 80-percent of all muzzleloading guns built and sold are of the modern in-line design. And it is the big game hunter looking for improved performance that has established that popularity.

The 250-grain .452" XTP has a ballistics coefficient of just .147. The jacketed hollow-point is about as aerodynamic as a flying ashtry! By the time 100 grains of Pyrodex gets the bullet to 100 yards, it has slowed to around 1,250 f.p.s. and hits with only about 860 f.p.e. At 150 yards, the load would be good for less than 600 foot-pounds of remaining energy. When a shooter loads a 150-grain charge of Pyrodex Pellets behind this bullet and sabot, out of a 24-inch barrel the load is good for 1,955 f.p.s., with 2,125 f.p.e. Again, due to the low b.c. of the XTP hollow-point, at 100 yards velocity has dropped to around 1,520 f.p.s. with 1,280 f.p.e. retention. Out at 200 yards, the load would hit a whitetail with a little more than 725 f.p.e.

That extra 50-grain pellet produces 335 additional feet per second and 680 more foot-pounds of energy at the muzzle. In turn, this extends the effective range of the 250-grain Hornady XTP considerably.

A few years ago, Thompson/Center Arms regularly advertised their Encore 209x50 Magnum as "The Most Powerful .50 cal. Muzzleloader in the World!" claiming that the rifle, loaded with a 150-grain charge of Pyrodex Pellets and a saboted 240-grain bullet, was capable of producing "Muzzle energy equal to a 7mm Rem. Mag." The company stated in their advertising that the load was good for 2,203 f.p.s. at the muzzle of the 26-inch barrel. Now, according to my calculations, a bullet of this weight at that muzzle velocity would only generate about 2,580 f.p.e.—not the 3,100 to 3,200 f.p.e. produced by most 7mm Remington Magnum factory loads.

Curious, I have conducted several ballistics sessions with the break-open T/C muzzleloader and several other 26-inch barreled and No. 209 primer ignited in-line muzzleloaders to see if I could duplicate the company's published ballistics. One of those rifles was

THE HIGH COST OF HIGH PERFORMANCE

Have you really ever sat down and studied exactly what it costs to get the level of performance you seek from your modern in-line muzzleloading rifle and high performance load? If you are shooting the latest in muzzleloader bullet technology, and with the "magnum" loads of Pyrodex or Triple Seven Pellets, you just might be amazed at what a few more feet per second or a few more added foot-pounds of energy can set you back. And to some degree, the cost per shot may affect how much shooting you can afford to do during the course of each year.

When shopping for my first muzzle-loaded deer rifle back in 1963, I spent a great deal of time thumbing through the DIixie Gun Works catalog. I remember reading how the company's founder, the late Turner Kirkland, was able to shoot the original guns he bought during the 1930s (for $10 to $15) for just 3 to 4 cents per shot by casting his own round ball projectiles, using scrap cotton for patching and even occasionally making his own percussion caps out of metal salvaged from "tin cans" and caps for toy guns. More to ensure a supply of shootable round balls for my first muzzleloader (a percussion Dixie .45 caliber Kentucky rifle) than to save money, I also cast my own round balls for the front-loader. Back then, a pound of FFFg black powder cost me less than $5, and a tin of 100 percussion caps was around $1.25. Again, like ol' Turner, I generally used heavy cotton material scraps for patching those 128-grain .440" soft lead round balls. And the loads I used for the first time on whitetails during the 1964 Illinois season cost me around 10 to 12 cents per shot.

THINGS CERTAINLY HAVE CHANGED SINCE THOSE DAYS!

Next time you're in your local gun shop, take a few minutes to just look at the retail prices of today's high performance muzzleloading components. Loading and shooting many of today's more advanced in-line rifle models with the loads recommended by the manufacturer can now cost you more than shooting a big-bore center-fire rifle chambered for cartridges like the .375 H&H Magnum or the .458 Winchester Magnum!

Most of the current "Premium" bullets with sabots retail for at least $15 per pack of ten, and some sell for as high as $20 for 10 bullets and sabots. That's $1.50 to $2.00 per shot—FOR JUST THE BULLET AND SABOT! And if you're one of those shooters who have gone to a hefty 150-grain (black powder equivalent) pelletized powder charge, either for the added speed and knockdown power or for the convenience, you are also paying 75 to 80 cents per shot for propellant. On top of all that, some current models, like the H&R "Huntsman" or the Knight D.I.S.C. and D.I.S.C. Extreme models, require the use of a specialized primer carrier that can add upward of 10 cents per shot. And when the cost of a No. 209 primer or even a No. 11 percussion cap or musket cap is factored in, many of today's more widely used loads cost from around $2.30 to right at $3.00—EACH AND EVERY TIME THE TRIGGER IS PULLED.

At those prices, how many rounds can you justify shooting through the course of a year? The muzzleloading hunter who shoots just 200 shots annually could have more money invested in loading and shooting components in just the first year than the price paid for the rifle itself.

If the popularity of high performance muzzleloading big game rifles is to continue, component makers must get a handle on the outrageous investment it takes to tap the full potential of these front-loaders. Not many enjoy owning a rifle they cannot afford to get out and shoot often enough to know just how it performs at 50...100...150...or 200 yards.

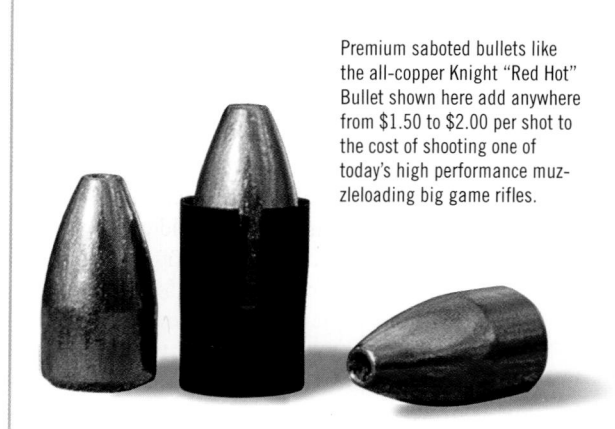

Premium saboted bullets like the all-copper Knight "Red Hot" Bullet shown here add anywhere from $1.50 to $2.00 per shot to the cost of shooting one of today's high performance muzzleloading big game rifles.

the Lenartz Rdi-50, the other a custom barreled Savage Model 10ML II. The highest velocity I could attain with a magnum charge of Pyrodex Pellets and a saboted .452" Hornady 240-grain XTP-MAG bullet was 2,020 f.p.s.—and that was with a 180-grain charge!

The Model 10ML II, at this writing, was the only production in-line muzzleloader designed and built to allow the use of modern nitrocellulose-based smokeless powders. The No. 209 primer ignition system of this rifle is as efficient as that of the T/C Encore 209x50 Magnum, maybe even slightly more efficient. Since the Savage rifle is built to stand up to pressures two…three…four times that produced by 150-grain Pyrodex Pellet charges, I decided to see how heavy a Pyrodex Pellet load it would take to get that saboted 240-grain bullet out of the muzzle at 2,203 f.p.s.!

Connecticut Valley Arms was one of the first companies to follow Knight's lead with the in-line ignition rifles. Shown here is their first in-line model, the Apollo.

With three of the 50-grain pellets behind the sabot and bullet, the rifle produced a velocity of just 1,973 f.p.s. When I attempted to load four of the 50-grain pellets, I saw very little jump in velocity, but a whole lot in recoil. Three consecu-

tive shots across the chronograph gave me an average velocity of 1,988 f.p.s. Then I loaded with three 50-grain pellets and one 30-grain pellet, for a 180-grain charge, and got up to the 2,020 f.p.s. quoted earlier. I concluded that, out of a 26-inch barreled and primer ignited in-line rifle, it was impossible to get a saboted 240-grain bullet out of the muzzle at 2,203 f.p.s.—no matter how many Pyrodex Pellets were loaded behind the sabot and bullet.

Still curious to see if I could get a saboted bullet out of the Savage muzzleloader at 2,200+ f.p.s., I went to Triple Seven Pellets and FFFg Triple Seven. Now, it should be noted here that Hodgdon Powder Company lists a 100-grain charge of either Triple Seven, pellets or loose grain, as their "Recommended Maximum Load." Again, since the Savage Model 10ML II had been built to withstand far greater pressures, I felt safe moving the amount of powder loaded behind a saboted 240-grain bullet on up the line. With four Triple Seven Pellets (200-grain black powder equivalent load), I could only get 2,080 f.p.s. Three of the pellets gave me

2,027 f.p.s. with a lot less recoil. However, with 140 grains of FFFg Triple Seven, I finally got a saboted 240-grain bullet out of the muzzle at 2,207 f.p.s.. The load was good for 2,700 f.p.e. and proved capable of printing 100-yard three-shot groups of around 1½-inches. (Read more about the Savage Model 10ML II and the smokeless powder loads that perform well out of this rifle in the following chapter.)

Today's modern in-line ignition muzzleloading rifles are capable of shooting faster, flatter and harder than any muzzle-loaded big game rifles of the past. However, in their quests to remain competitive, many manufacturers are now claiming performance that the consumer simply will not be able to duplicate.

In recent years, there has been a resurgence of interest in shooting the .45 caliber rifles. During the 1960s and early 1970s, rifles of this bore size reigned in popularity. However, only a handful of states actually conducted a special "muzzleloader only" big game season back then, and the vast majority of interest in muzzleloading was shooting targets with patched round ball loads. As the separate muzzleloading seasons and hunts continued to grow in popularity, the smaller bore .45 quickly lost

Author Toby Bridges with a fine late-season muzzleloader whitetail, taken with a .50 caliber Knight thumbhole-stocked LK-93 "Wolverine" and saboted 260-grain Speer .451" jacketed hollow-point bullet.

ground to the more effective .50 and .54 caliber rifles.

Turning to a new and better selection of saboted .40 and .357 caliber bullets, Knight Rifles, Thompson/Center Arms, Traditions, Connecticut Valley Arms and a few others have sparked new interest in hunting with a .45 caliber in-line rifle. With today's powders, some of these in-lines are now capable of getting a sub 200-grain bullet out of the muzzle at around 2,500 f.p.s., with extremely mild recoil and outstanding accuracy. Other companies, like White and Gonic have gone the other way, turning to long, heavy lead conical bullets to turn the fast-twist .45 caliber rifles into deadly accurate 200-yard big game rifles.

In 2003, Knight Rifles introduced their D.I.S.C. Extreme model in an all-new .52 caliber in an attempt to establish a new niche. Muzzleload Magnum Products developed two new sabots for the bore, one that allows .458" diameter bullets to be loaded, the other using bullets of .475" diameter. Knight's goal was to offer a harder hitting bore size for the elk hunter, relying on 150-grain charges of loose-grain Triple Seven and bullets of 350 to 400 grains.

Still, the .50 caliber continues to reign in popularity, and the muzzleloading hunter will find an almost mind boggling variety of outstanding hunting projectiles available, both saboted and bore size. In this book you will find chapters devoted to each of today's most popular calibers, along with chapters on saboted bullets and full-bore diameter conical lead bullets. The information in each of these chapters is sure to help any modern in-line rifle shooter make a more informed choice.

Thompson/Center Arms is one of today's leading in-line ignition rifle manufacturers, with nearly a half-dozen different models to choose from. This hunter used one of the very popular T/C Encore 209x50 Magnum break-open rifles to take this great buck.

New in-line ignition big game rifles continue to be introduced almost annually. Whether or not the ignition systems found on some of these are any better than the systems found on rifles already available may take several seasons to prove or disprove. More than likely, it will be other features that will ultimately determine whether these rifles are a success or not. Like the simple dropping action of the Thompson/Center Arms "Omega" or the longer barrel of newer break-open designs like the Connecticut Valley Arms "Optima Pro."

Let's face it, muzzleloading today is more performance driven than at any other time in history. As we head on into the 21st Century, more and more modern technology will find its way into this centuries-old shooting sport. No one really knows where all of this technology will end. The consumer is the one in control and manufacturers generally respond to their demands. The muzzleloading rifle maker who fails to bring to the market exactly what the shooter and hunter wants won't be around for long.

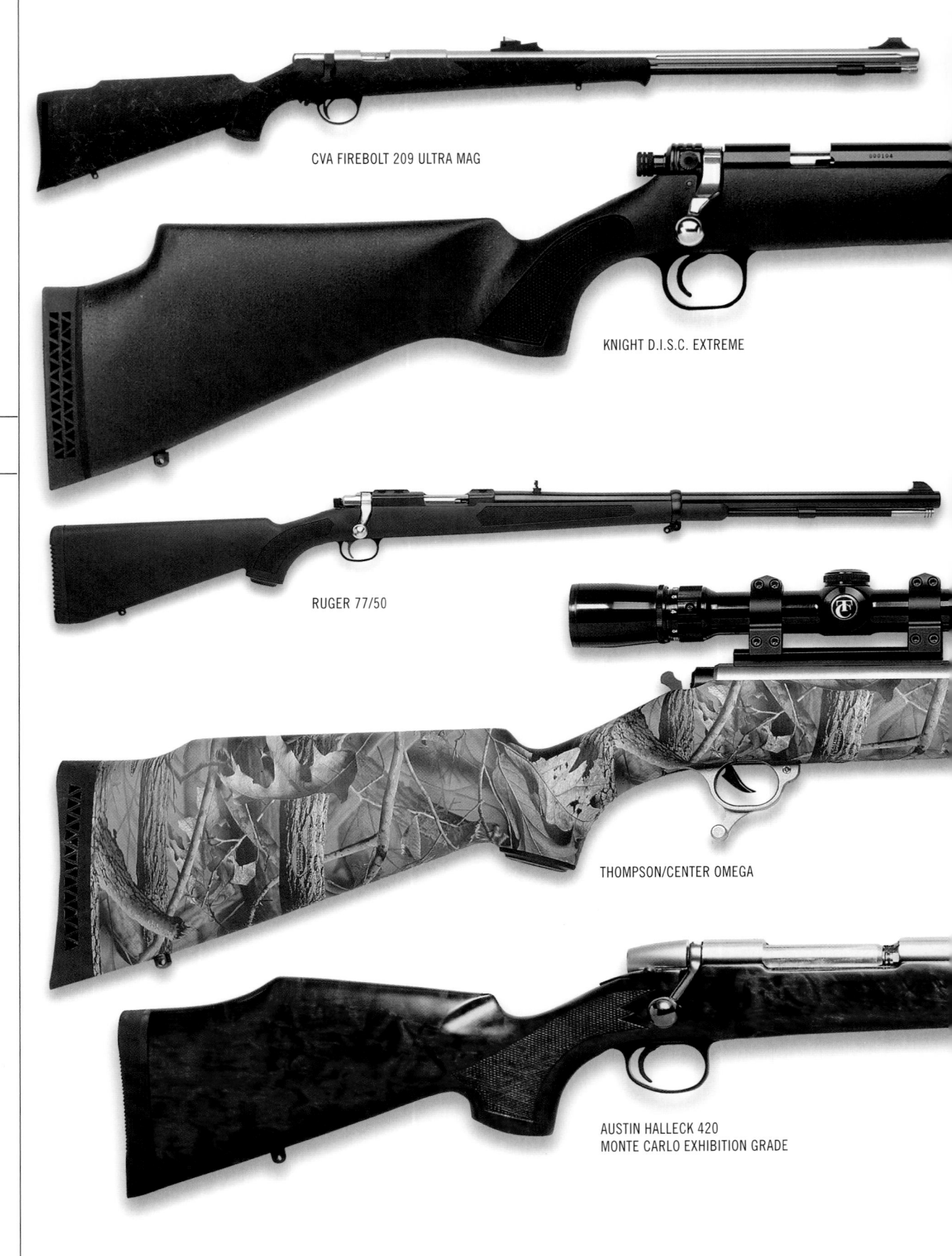

CVA FIREBOLT 209 ULTRA MAG

KNIGHT D.I.S.C. EXTREME

RUGER 77/50

THOMPSON/CENTER OMEGA

AUSTIN HALLECK 420
MONTE CARLO EXHIBITION GRADE

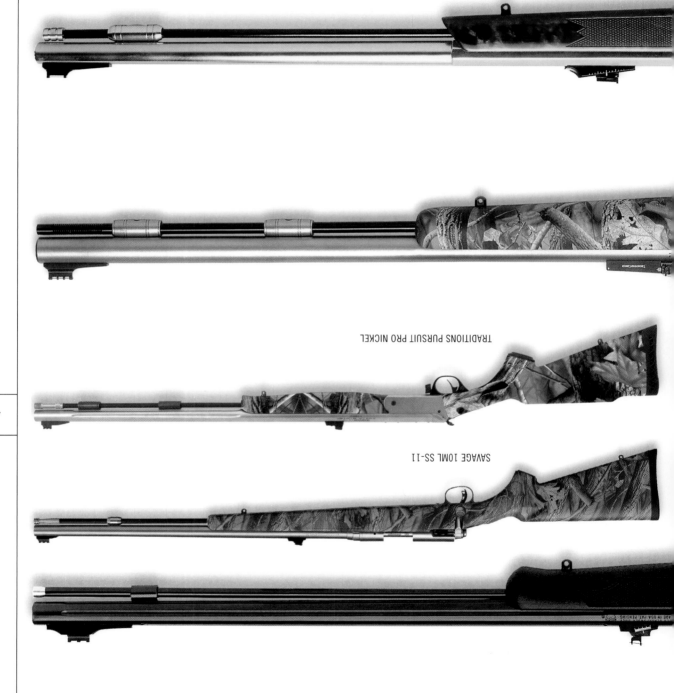

TRADITIONS PURSUIT PRO NICKEL

SAVAGE 10ML SS-II

the birth of
SMOKELESS MUZZLELOADING

Not one of the ultra modern in-line percussion ignition rifles covered in the previous chapter could ever be considered a "traditional" muzzleloading rifle. Yet, the rifle models just detailed, along with dozens of other models built with most of the same features, are now the best-selling style of front-loaded hunting rifle. Likewise, they have become the most widely used during the special "muzzleloader only" seasons now enjoyed by tens of thousands of hunters in just about every state. (A growing number of states are now home to more than 100,000 muzzleloading big game hunters.)

Muzzleloader hunting regulations across the country continue to change rapidly to allow hunters to use the latest technology. Even so, many hunters are still faced with outdated regulations that mandate the use of less than ideal sighting systems or ineffective projectile designs. Fortunately, many departments have come to realize that muzzleloader hunting is no longer simply a nostalgic interest, and now leave the choice of modern or traditional entirely up to the individual hunter.

During one big game season or another, modern in-line percussion rifles, telescopic sights, saboted bullets and pelletized powders are now legal in the majority of states. Even Pennsylvania, known for decades for its very restrictive "Flintlock Only" December muzzleloading deer season, has now added an earlier season that permits practically any front-loaded rifle, projectile, sighting system, source of ignition or type of powder.

When it comes to modern-day muzzleloading, only one thing has remained constant, and that has been change. The rifles and loads preferred by today's muzzleloader toting hunter are a far cry from the long-barreled frontloaders and fodder carried into the wilderness by the likes of Daniel Boone and Jim Bridger. And even with all of the modern developments introduced to the muzzleloading market over the past couple of decades, the sport will surely continue to change. In fact, it is now facing one of the biggest changes ever, the introduction of muzzleloaders built to consume loads of better performing and cleaner burning nitrocellulose-based "smokeless powders."

During the spring of 2000, Savage Arms Inc. (Westfield, Massachusetts) boldly moved into territory where no other muzzleloading rifle manufacturer has ever trespassed. The company tooled up and began producing their Model 10ML II—the first production muzzleloader ever designed, engineered and built to be loaded and shot with modern smokeless powders.

FAR LEFT: The Savage Model 10ML II has raised the bar for muzzleloader performance once more. This rifle gets its zip and performance from the hot smokeless powder loads it shoots well. The author took this Nebraska buck at 214 yards with his Savage "smokeless pole."

Using any nitrocellulose-based powder in any gun that loaded from the front has always been strictly taboo. These powders, which are used to load ammunition for modern center-fire rifles, handguns and shotguns, simply produce pressures that are far too excessive for conventional in-line ignition and traditionally styled muzzleloaders. However, thanks to a revolutionary new concept in muzzleloader ignition systems, Savage Arms becomes the first manufacturer to harness the energy and user-friendliness of modern smokeless powders. And the innovative Savage Model 10ML II does it without placing shooter's safety in danger.

The concept around which Savage has built their innovative front-loader is the brainchild of Henry Ball, a custom rifle maker from Greensboro, North Carolina. The heart of his system is a modern center-fire action, and Ball has favored the strength of a good bolt-action receiver over actions of any other type. His original smokeless muzzleloader was built on a short Interarms Mark-X action, to which he installed a .50 caliber McGowen barrel. Like most other in-line ignition muzzleloaders, Ball's custom rifles feature a removable breech plug. However, instead of a nipple, the breech plug of this system features a chamber that accepts a reusable stainless steel ignition module primed with a hot No. 209 shotshell primer.

To constrict the fire from the primer, and to prevent granules of powder filtering back into the chamber area, plus to keep the pressures created by smokeless powders from escaping to the rear, Ball's patented design relies on a tiny .030" orifice running through a removable vent liner positioned between the chamber and the powder area of the barrel. When one of his stainless steel ignition modules is chambered in the rifle, 100 percent of the fire from a No. 209 primer passes through the orifice and into the barrel for guaranteed ignition. The extremely precise fit of the module in the chamber also makes this system exceptionally weatherproof.

Before the author had Henry Ball build him one of his custom smokeless muzzleloaders in 1997, I had an opportunity to fire several thousand rounds through a variety of rifles he had built, including rifles built on Sako, Howa, Remington and Interarms Mauser actions. Since, I have seen a few other Ball rifles built on Remington rolling-block, Martini dropping-block and H&R break-open actions, plus one beautiful smokeless muzzleloader he built on a Ruger No. 1 single-shot action.

While this system can be loaded and shot with charges of black powder, Pyrodex, Pyrodex Pellets, Triple Seven and Triple Seven Pellets, plus any other black powder substitute, these rifles have been designed to perform best with loads of modern nitrocellulose-based smokeless powders. And for someone who has been writing about muzzleloading since the early 1970s, always warning readers to "NEVER SHOOT SMOKELESS POWDER" in any muzzleloader, it was with great reservation that I sat down at the bench and touched off my first few shots with the smokeless powder loads recommended by Henry Ball.

My initial shooting was done with a load favored by the rifle's maker—33 grains of Alliant 2400 behind a saboted 260-grain Speer .451" jacketed hollowpoint. The first three shots out of Ball's original Mark-X actioned rifle printed well inside of 1½ inches at 100 yards, and the chronograph revealed that the bul-

North Carolina custom riflemaker Henry Ball is the man behind the new smokeless muzzleloading concept. Here, he holds a beautiful custom .45 smokeless front-loader he built on a Sako action.

Ball's first bolt-action smokeless muzzleloader was built on an Interams Mini-Mark-X action. This 1¼-inch, 100-yard group is typical of the accuracy the rifle would consistently produce.

let was leaving the muzzle at almost 2,200 f.p.s. My second group was even better. Best of all, there was no need to wipe fouling from the bore between shots, or to tear down the rifle and scrub fouling from the bore and other metal parts at the end of the shooting session. The very low recoil of the smokeless loads was equally impressive.

During the fall of 1997, I hunted with a custom Ball .50 caliber smokeless muzzleloader built for me on a Howa bolt-action receiver. That rifle shot extremely well with a 45-grain charge of IMR-4227 behind a Muzzleload Magnum Products sabot and 250-grain .452" Hornady XTP jacketed hollow-point bullet. At 100 yards, the rifle and load would consistently print inside of an inch, and several of the better groups shot could be covered with a quarter. At the muzzle, the load is good for just over 2,100 f.p.s. and generates a little more than 2,500 f.p.e. I cleanly dropped several good bucks that fall with the rifle. One, a wide-racked eight-pointer, gave me a shot at about 200 yards, and at the crack of the rifle that deer literally dropped in its tracks.

Savage Steps Up to the Plate

It was during the last half of 1999 that Savage Arms first caught wind of Henry Ball's unique muzzleloading system. For some time, the company had been eyeing the muzzleloader market, but with superb bolt-action designs like the Remington Model 700ML and the Ruger Model 77/50 already available, Savage felt there wasn't enough demand for another look alike, perform alike front-loader of similar design and capabilities. But after shooting a .50 caliber rifle Ball had built for Savage on one of the company's Model 110 FP Tactical Rifle actions, Savage C.E.O. Ron Coburn and his staff immediately realized that this was truly a design that was anything but muzzleloading as usual.

The following spring, Savage built a limited run of prototype rifles, utilizing Ball's ignition module concept. One of the first 12 prototypes was sent to me to wring out, and I immediately knew the company had a winner on their hands. The Savage-produced smokeless muzzleloaders performed as well as any of the Ball custom rifles I had shot.

For the 7¾-pound production run .50 caliber Model 10ML rifles, Savage elected to use a modified version of their short Model 12 single-shot varmint/target action. The difference between this and other Savage center-fire rifle actions is the "single-shot" aspect. Missing on this action is the ejector that could flip an ignition module into tall grass, as well as the cutout in the bottom of the receiver for a magazine. The stainless steel ignition module has to be pushed into the chamber (with a finger) and the bolt closed behind it.

Enter the Revamped Model 10ML II

In 2001, Savage modified the action to eliminate the use of the module, which some shooters didn't like. While the modules could each be reused several hundred times before the fit became loose enough to allow a minute amount of gas leakage, the shooter did have to take a decapping pin and knock the spent primer from the module, then re-prime by pushing a new 209 primer in with a thumb. At the shooting bench, the process took about 15 seconds or less. When in the field, hunters carrying a Model 10ML would simply pack along a half-dozen primed modules for the day's hunt.

Muzzleloading hunter Don Oster couldn't wait until the whitetail season in his home state of Indiana to try out his new Savage Model 10ML II, so he booked an exotic hunt for Axis deer. He dropped the big buck where it stood at 100 yards with a single 250-grain Hornady SST that left the muzzle at almost 2,400 f.p.s.

The revised Savage smokeless muzzleloader has been dubbed the Model 10ML II. Instead of a chamber for the ignition module, the breech plug of the Model 10ML II features a much smaller chamber for just the No. 209 shotgun primer. The bolt of the original Ball design featured the same bolt face as a standard center-fire design. The new bolt face of the Model 10ML II instead allows the shooter to slip the flanged shoulder of the primer into a "shell-holder" type of arrangement. When the bolt is closed, the primer is snugly pushed into the small chamber at the rear of the breech plug. When the handle is lifted and the bolt pulled rearward, the spent primer is extracted from the breech plug.

The current version of the rifle still utilizes Ball's patented replaceable vent liner. The hotter flame of a No. 209 primer does tend to erode the small orifice running through this sacrificial part much quicker than the flame produced by the No. 11 or musket caps used for ignition in many other in-line rifle models. Tests have shown that when shooting hot loads of smokeless powder, the orifice will burn out from its original .030" diameter to about .035" after just 50 to 60 shots. And by the time 100 shots have been fired through the tiny passageway, most loads will erode the passageway to around .038" to .040". Once the hole has enlarged to that point, accuracy will begin to open.

Another reason for Savage's decision to eliminate the ignition module was to make the Model 10ML II form No. 4473 exempt. The Bureau of Alcohol, Tobacco, and Firearms (BATF) had determined that since the original Model 10ML was built with a receiver and bolt that could possibly be converted into a modern cartridge firearm, buyers would have to fill out the form the same as for any modern center-fire cartridge rifle.

Missing on the newer Model 10ML II version are the locking lugs at the front of the bolt and the "bolt release" along the rear right side of the receiver. A screw running through from the trigger guard and the bolt handle itself now provides the "lock up" for the bolt. The tip of the long front trigger guard screw protrudes up through the bottom of the revamped receiver and rides in a milled groove along the bottom of the bolt. When the bolt is in the closed position, the handle turns down into a deep notch milled into the side of the receiver.

Every Savage muzzleloader comes with a breech plug wrench that's long enough to pass through the receiver and engage the notches at the rear of the breech plug. Ten or so counter clockwise turns with the wrench loosens the breech plug, allowing it to be slid rearward through the receiver and removed. To keep this breech plug, and the smaller vent liner, removable requires applying lube to the threads of both parts. Some Model 10ML II shooters prefer automotive anti-seize compounds, some use the lube applied to keep shotgun choke tubes easily removable.

Benefits of Smokeless Powder

Thanks to the noncorrosive nature of nitrocellulose-based smokeless powders, cleanup and maintenance of the Savage Model 10ML II (and earlier Model 10ML) is a cinch, requiring little more care than most center-fire bolt-action rifles. Between April and December 2000, I personally fired more than 4,000 rounds through the Model 10ML prototype Savage sent me to determine the compatible range of powders for the rifle, and which sabots and bullets turned in the best accuracy. On most days, I'd shoot about 50 rounds, and at the end of the shooting session I'd merely pull out the breech plug and vent liner, then re-lube the threads of these parts. Before installing these, I'd first run two or three nitro-solvent dampened patches through the bore. Cleanup normally took only about five minutes.

A muzzleloader that requires little cleaning and maintenance has long been the dream of most hunters. Too often, muzzleloading big game hunters who are successful during the last few hours of an evening hunt are faced with taking care of the game downed, getting the animal out of the field and often to a checking station, then onto the meat pole or to a processing plant. All of this must be done before time can usually be devoted to caring for the rifle used to harvest the game.

When shooting and hunting with loads comprised of either black powder or a black powder substitute such as Pyrodex, close and immediate attention to the rifle is mandatory. The fouling or residue left behind by these propellants is

ABOVE: Shown sitting inside the receiver of this Ball-built custom smokeless muzzleloader is one of the reusable ignition modules covered by his patents. The system relied on hot No. 209 shot-shell primers for 100 percent ignition of the smokeless loads.

ABOVE LEFT: The patented removable and replaceable vent liner of the Ball system allows shooters to economically replace a burnt-out or eroded vent orifice.

First-time muzzleloading hunter Deborah Bennett chose to use the author's custom Ball smokeless muzzleloader because of the low recoil and excellent accuracy. It also delivered plenty of knockdown for her first buck, which was dropped in its tracks by the saboted 250-grain Hornady XTP.

extremely corrosive. Under certain high humidity or damp weather conditions, fouling left in the bore overnight can totally ruin a high-quality muzzleloader.

Cleaning a dirty muzzleloader has, in fact, always been a major concern. In some cases, the apprehension of having to clean a gun of muzzleloading design has been strong enough to keep many modern-day shooters from ever getting involved with the sport. The new Savage Model 10ML II has all but eliminated the mess associated with shooting a front-loading rifle. Following a successful day in the deer woods, chasing elk or stalking any other big game animal, this rifle can be left a day…a week…or a month without having to scrub the bore or worry about ruining the rifle.

Since the late 1990s, Knight Rifles, Thompson/Center Arms and a few other muzzleloader manufacturers have heavily promoted the use of three 50-grain Pyrodex Pellet charges (150-grain load) behind modern saboted bullets for "magnum" big-game-taking performance. With such loads, Thompson/Center Arms has even proclaimed its Encore 209x50 Magnum break-open muzzleloader as the "World's Most Powerful .50 Caliber Muzzleloader." The company says that a 150-grain charge of Pyrodex Pellets behind a saboted 240-grain bullet is good for 2,200 f.p.s. at the muzzle, with muzzle energy equivalent to a 7mm Remington Magnum.

Savage's Model 10ML II can be loaded with any charge of black powder, Pyrodex or any other black powder substitute that can be loaded and fired in any other muzzleloader—with comparable ballistics. However, this rifle has the distinction of being the only production rifle currently available that can stand up to the pressures of modern smokeless powders. The three 50-grain Pyrodex Pellet charges used to give shooters magnum performance in other in-line ignition rifles generate internal barrel pressures of around 18,000 to 19,000 p.s.i. when shooting a saboted 250-grain bullet. Depending on the nitrocellulose-based powder loaded and shot, the Model 10ML II will push pressures up between 30,000 and 40,000 p.s.i. with the same weight bullet. These pressures are more than enough to destroy many of the other in-line models currently available.

Four powders that have been stellar performers out of the Savage muzzleloader have been IMR-4227 (or Hodgdon H-4227), Accurate Arms XMP5744, IMR-SR4759 and VihtaVuori N110. All four are short-cut extruded powders of the medium burn rate variety—i.e., a little slower than Alliant 2400 and a little faster than Alliant Reloder 7. Of the four, IMR-4227 is the slowest burning, VihtaVuori N110 the fastest burning.

My first three-shot group with the Savage Model 10ML prototype, shooting a 45-grain charge of IMR-4227 behind a saboted 300-grain .452" Hornady XTP hollow-point bullet, printed a tight cluster at 100 yards that was barely an inch across (center to center). The outside temperature was right at 50 degrees, and I gave the rifle about a five-minute cool-down between shots. Then, I allowed it to cool for about 15 minutes before shooting my second group with the rifle and load. That group was equally tight.

This was also the first time for Muzzleload Magnum Products' new high pressure sabot to be shot with smokeless loads. While the company had developed the sabot to withstand the pressures of 150-grain Pyrodex Pellet charges, the improved configuration of the sabot base and the tougher polymer used in its construction also stood up to the still higher pressures generated by the smokeless loads. At the time, a 45-grain charge of IMR-4227 was the hottest load that could be shot without blowing a standard pressure sabot. Shooting the Model 10ML prototype, I found that I could work loads up to 48 grains without damaging the new sabot. That charge was good for 2,175 f.p.s. with the 300-grain XTP, topping 3,100 f.p.e.

Shooting the lighter 250-grain Hornady bullet of the same diameter, the Model 10ML produced an honest muzzle velocity of just over 2,250 f.p.s. and generated just over 2,800 f.p.e.

While it may seem contrary to logic, or basic physics for that matter, the smokeless loads that produce higher velocities and greater energy levels than possible with the three 50-grain Pyrodex Pellet charges do so with far less recoil. Thanks to the lack of dirty fouling left in the bore by each and every shot, as with Pyrodex, this system tends to produce better than average accuracy with less effort by the shooter. With either the 300- or 250-grain XTP and Muzzleload Magnum Products high pressure sabot, the Savage Model 10ML prototype consistently proved capable of printing nice 1- to 1½-inch groups at 100 yards.

Is the Savage the Strongest Muzzleloader Built?

During the heat of that first summer shooting the new Model 10ML II, I quickly discovered one thing about those hot smokeless loads fired from the Savage muzzleloader. Once temperatures climb into the upper 80s or 90s, accuracy with near maximum loads begins to suffer. The high pressure Muzzleload Magnum Products sabots have proven to be the best for shooting with smokeless loads out of this rifle. However, these sabots were developed for the 150-grain Pyrodex Pellet loads, which develop just under 20,000 p.s.i. The smokeless loads fired in the Model 10ML II produce internal barrel pressures that can top 40,000 p.s.i., which is about the same breech pressure produced by hot loads in a .444 Marlin. In the world of center-fire cartridges, the pressures and velocities produced by the Savage muzzleloader would be considered on the low side. However, in the world of modern in-line muzzleloading rifles, such pressures and velocities are definitely on the high side.

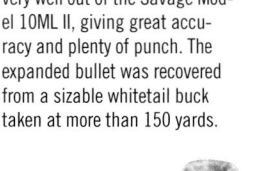

The Hornady .452" diameter 250-grain XTP has performed very well out of the Savage Model 10ML II, giving great accuracy and plenty of punch. The expanded bullet was recovered from a sizable whitetail buck taken at more than 150 yards.

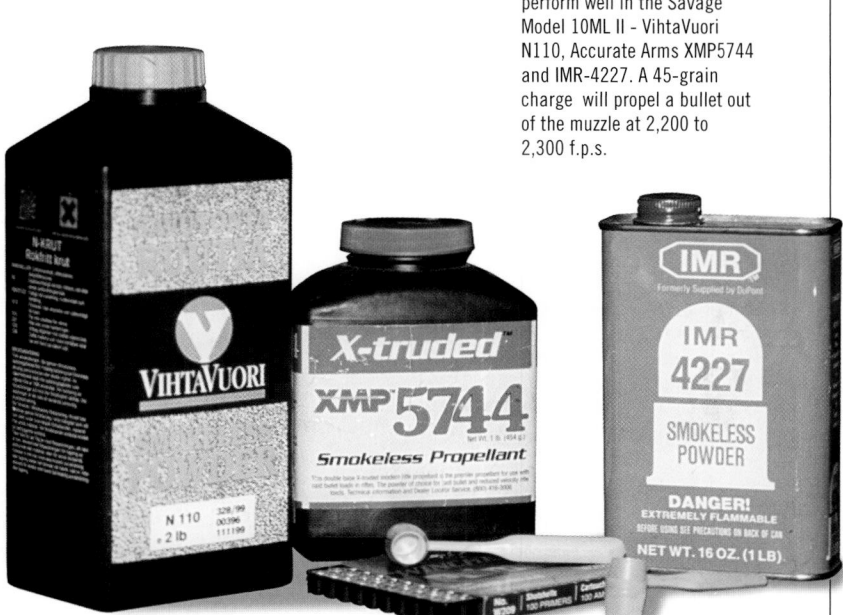

Three smokeless powders that perform well in the Savage Model 10ML II - VihtaVuori N110, Accurate Arms XMP5744 and IMR-4227. A 45-grain charge will propel a bullet out of the muzzle at 2,200 to 2,300 f.p.s.

While the management at Savage won't readily share with the shooting public to what pressures they have tested this innovative muzzleloader, they will share that they have done their darndest to destruct one of the rifles. So far, they have failed. And these tests have been conducted with multiple smokeless powder charges under multiple saboted bullets.

Now, this doesn't mean a shooter can add as much powder as he pleases, just that this muzzleloader has been built to withstand pressures far greater than any other muzzleloader ever offered. Once pressures reach into the upper 40,000 p.s.i. range, the sabot generally cannot stand up to the jolt and comes apart. When it does, much of that contained pressure escapes around the bullet and exits the muzzle. In a sense, the sabot is also the pressure relief valve of the Model 10ML II.

The hottest powder I've shot in the Model 10ML II and still achieved accuracy has been IMR-SR4756. Loading just 28-grain charges of this powder, I've managed to get a saboted 180-grain Knight "Red Hot" bullet out of the 24-inch .50 caliber barrel at around 2,290 f.p.s. Three-shot groups fired with this load typically would average around 1½ inches across when temperatures were in the 60s or lower. However, when attempts were made to shoot with slightly slower burning Alliant Blue Dot, a charge of just 20 grains would completely destroy the sabot every time. I ran into the same thing when trying to work up loads with Hodgdon HS-6, which is also slightly slower burning than IMR-SR4756.

Author Toby Bridges with the very first head of big game ever harvested with the Savage Model 10ML muzzleloader prototype. The wild Texas porker was dropped where it stood.

The physical characteristics of the granules tend to play an extremely important role in whether or not a particular smokeless powder will perform out of the Model 10ML II. Blue Dot granules are flat flakes, and HS-6 is a "rolled" powder, or spherical "ball" powder that has been somewhat flattened into a disc. The powders that tend to work well in the Savage smokeless system are primarily short-cut extruded medium burn rate powders with granules that are approximately .035 to .040 inch in length.

The two best performing smokeless powders the author has shot through his Model 10ML II rifles have been VihtaVuori N110 and IMR-SR4759. These two powders have given some of the best accuracy with a wide variety of saboted bullets, and at velocities exceeding 2,300 f.p.s. Of the two powders, VihtaVuori N110 is the hotter powder. Still, I've found that I can shoot heavier charges with this powder than with IMR-SR4759.

A 44.5-grain charge of VihtaVuori N110 will get a saboted 250-grain bullet from the muzzle at 2,368 f.p.s., with right at 3,100 f.p.e. Best groups are shot when temperatures are in the 40s and 50s. Even then, it is imperative that the barrel be given about a five-minute cooldown between shots. When the time is taken to ensure a precise powder charge, to use the same amount of seating pressure on the sabot and bullet, and when the barrel is allowed to cool fully, this load has consistently rewarded me with tight 1-inch groups.

A 43-grain charge of IMR-SR4759 is about all I've been able to load behind a saboted 250- or 300-grain bullet without blowing or damaging the skirt of an MMP high-pressure sabot. Using an RCBS digital electronic scale, the coarse-grained IMR-SR4759 weighs up nicely. Precisely measured 43-grain charges have performed well behind a number of different saboted bullets. With the saboted 250-grain Hornady XTP, accuracy is every bit as good as with N110. The slightly

lighter charge does result in slightly slower velocities, getting the 250-grain hollow-point out of the muzzle at 2,335 f.p.s. That translates into 3,025 f.p.e. No other .50 caliber muzzleloader, past or present, can match this game-taking performance.

The slightly smaller granules of VihtaVuori N110 makes the powder ideal for measuring with the Lee Precision plastic dippers. While these charges are not as precise as charges measured on a good electronic scale, they are usually within two-tenths of a grain. The 3.7cc Lee dipper will measure, on the average, a 44.4-grain dose of N110. Velocity with the charge behind a 250-grain bullet is right at 2,360 f.p.s., and accuracy with the dipper measured charge is still usually well under 2 inches at 100 yards. The Lee Precision dippers are a great way to quickly measure hunting charges.

One advantage of IMR-SR4759 over VihtaVuori N110 is that the powder can be purchased in ½-pound cans, while the smallest container of N110 available is a 2-pound canister. The "cost per shot" for either powder is very comparable. However, a ½-pound can of SR4759 can be bought for about one-quarter the cost of a 2-pound container of N110. This means that a shooter who puts in only about a hundred shots a year through the Model 10ML II is more likely to have a can of fresh powder for each season. Shooting 43-grain charges, a half-pound can of SR4759 will give a shooter 81 shots.

ABOVE LEFT: Shooters are finding the smokeless loads fired out of the Savage muzzleloader to give higher velocities, greater energy levels and flatter trajectory, but with a lot less recoil and much easier clean-up.

ABOVE: Without all of the fuss and mess generally associated with muzzleloading, the new Savage smokeless front-loader puts some fun back into muzzle-load-er shooting.

Innovation Brings about Change

The higher pressures and improved ballistics of the Savage Model 10ML II have already begun to bring about changes with the components we load and shoot. Muzzleload Magnum Products has already greatly improved the design and strength of the plastic sabot. And since the Savage muzzleloader has hit the mar-

Today's muzzleloading hunter wants a rifle that can deliver optimum knockdown and great accuracy without a lot of work. The Savage Model 10ML II delivers.

ket, several bullet makers have introduced new projectiles that will better tap the downrange performance of this hard-hitting muzzle-loaded big game rifle.

In 2002, Parker Productions, of Spring Creek, Nevada, introduced a new jacketed, spire-point version of their "Hydra-Con" bullet that is proving to be an excellent performer out of this rifle. That fall, I used the .451- inch, 250-, 275- and 300-grain Parker bullets to harvest 14 whitetails, including three that were shot at just over 200 yards. All but two of those deer went down on the spot. The two "runners" went less than 20 yards before going down.

During the early spring of 2003, Hornady Manufacturing Company sent me a supply of their new polymer-tipped SST bullets to test with smokeless loads in the Model 10ML II. The .452" diameter, 250- and 300-grain spire-point bullets shot superbly with the same powder charges that performed well behind the company's jacketed hollow-point XTP bullets. However, thanks to the vastly improved aerodynamics and increased ballistic coefficient of the SST design, this bullet will deliver far more knockdown power out at the outer limits of muzzle-loader effectiveness than possible with a blunt-nosed hollow-point bullet.

One of my favorite whitetail hunting loads for the Model 10ML II has been 44.5 grains of VihtaVuori N110 behind a saboted 250-grain Hornady XTP. As already pointed out, the load gets the bullet out of the muzzle at 2,368 f.ps., with 3,112 f.p.e. Now, this bullet has a ballistic coefficient of just .147. Due to the poor aerodynamics of the bullet, by the time it reaches 200 yards, it has slowed to around 1,375 f.p.s. and will hit a whitetail with about 1,050 f.p.e. of remaining energy. It's still more than enough to get the job done.

Hornady's new 250-grain SST has a ballistic coefficient of .240. With the same 44.5-grain charge of N110, the bullet leaves the muzzle at basically the same velocity and with the same energy as the 250-grain XTP hollow-point. However, thanks to the sleeker aerodynamics, this bullet does a much better job of retaining velocity and energy downrange. At 200 yards, the spire-point projectile will still be flying at close to 1,750 f.p.s., and hits its target with right at 1,700 foot-pounds of whitetail-taking energy.

The heftier 300-grain SST has a ballistic coefficient of around .295. Loaded ahead of 44.5 grains of VihtaVuori N110, the big bullet will leave the muzzle of the Model 10ML II at 2,244 f.p.s., generating a whopping 3,354 f.p.e. At 200 yards, the polymer-tipped spire-point drives home with just over 1,900 foot-pounds of knockdown power. TALK ABOUT AN ELK LOAD!

These polymer-tipped Hornady SST bullets bring center-fire rifle bullet technology to muzzleloading. The recovered bullet was taken from a large buck dropped at 100 yards.

Smokeless muzzleloading may not be for everyone, but it will appeal to the hunter looking for the hardest-hitting muzzle-loaded big game rifle available. Following a day of shooting or hunting, the noncorrosive nature of nitrocellulose-based powders cut rifle cleanup to just a few minutes. Plus that cleanup can safely be put off for a day or two without destroying the bore or mechanics of the rifle. And for the shooter on a tight budget, but who likes to shoot, smokeless muzzleloading delivers optimum game-taking performance and accuracy for about half the cost of shooting most other high performance muzzleloading big game rifles with magnum loads of Pyrodex Pellets or Triple Seven Pellets.

Innovation forces change, and just as the standard in-line percussion rifles changed the way hunters have looked at muzzleloading since the mid-1980s, the Savage smokeless Model 10ML II will change the way muzzleloading hunters think about muzzleloader performance as we head on into the 21st Century. Currently, Savage Arms is the only manufacturer to market a front-loader with smokeless powder capability, but they'll surely not be the last.

A small company in Hartford City, Indiana, that goes by the name of Smokeless Muzzleloading Inc. presently markets a replacement muzzle-loaded rifle barrel for the H&R break-open single-shot shotguns. The system has been designed to be loaded with slower burning smokeless powders, like IMR-4831. While velocities are slightly slower than possible with the powders compatible for the Savage Model 10ML II, a shooter can still enjoy the nearly maintenance-free operation and lower cost-per-shot economics of using smokeless powders.

Smokeless muzzleloading is here to stay, and it's only a matter of time before other manufacturers introduce other smokeless muzzle-loaded big game rifles.

the saboted muzzle-loaded
HUNTING
PROJECTILE

It takes just one look at almost any of the extremely modern in-line ignition muzzleloading rifles covered in the previous chapters to realize that these rifles have been designed with performance in mind. We're not only talking about vastly improved velocities and energy levels, but superior accuracy as well. And to tap the game-taking performance of these modern front-loaders generally requires loading a projectile…or rather projectile system…that's equally advanced.

The heart of each of these models or types is a sure-fire ignition system that guarantees fast and positive combustion of the powder charge—whether it's traditional black powder, Pyrodex, Triple Seven, one of the newer black powder substitutes, or in the case of the Savage Model 10ML II, "smokeless" powder. A majority of the best-selling models now incorporate modern center-fire rifle-like stocks, along with other modern features, such as safeties, fiberoptic sights and receivers that come drilled and tapped for easy installation of telescopic sights.

It's easy to see that these rifles have been built to deliver pinpoint accuracy. However, instead of loading and shooting traditional round ball or bore-sized lead conical projectiles from the past, today's muzzleloading hunter has turned to a projectile system that's as modern as the muzzleloader he or she now packs into the field. The muzzle-loaded hunting projectile of choice these days has become a modern jacketed or all-copper bullet that's loaded into the rifle with a tight-fitting plastic sabot.

Less than three decades ago, muzzleloaders with rifling that spun with one complete revolution in anything quicker than 48 inches was considered to have a fast rate of twist. Today, a one turn-in-48 inches rate of twist is considered slow. Muzzleloading rifle manufacturers have found that optimum accuracy with a plastic-saboted bullet is best achieved with relatively shallow rifling having a rate of twist as fast as one turn-in-20 to 28 inches. And the bores of nearly all modern in-line ignition rifles feature .003- to .005-inch-deep grooves that spiral at those stepped-up rates for best accuracy with the sabot system.

A .50 caliber Knight in-line rifle comes with a turn-in-28 inches twist; Gonic Arms relies on a slightly faster turn-in-24 inches in both .45 and .50 caliber models; Remington and Ruger in-line models feature rifling with a turn-in-28 inches; and the .50 caliber Savage Model 10ML II "smokeless powder" muzzleloader comes with a snappy one turn-in-24 inches rate of rifling twist. Some of the more recent "Super" .45 caliber in-line ignition models come with rifling that

FAR LEFT: Saboted bullets overcame early criticism about their effectiveness on bigger game and became the most widely used muzzle-loaded hunting projectile. Toby Bridges dropped this near 900-pound bull elk with a single 300-grain Barnes all-copper Expander MZ.

spins as fast as a turn-in-20 to 22 inches.

In the not-so-distant past, a few manufacturers offered in-line models with rates of twist as slow as one turn-in-32 to 38 inches. However, shooters found that these "slower" rates of twist often failed to properly stabilize longer bullet designs, especially all-copper bullets like the deeply hollow-point Barnes Expander MZ.

The sabot concept is really nothing new. It has been around for ages. In its simplest form, a sabot is almost anything that allows an undersized projectile to be loaded into and fired from a larger diameter bore. The sabot simply takes up the void between the smaller diameter projectile and larger bore. In fact, the cloth patch used to grip both a smaller diameter soft lead round ball and the rifling grooves of a traditionally styled muzzleloader bore is in essence a sabot. Saboted projectiles have been loaded and fired from cannon for hundreds of years. Saboted shotgun slugs have been around for more than 30 years. And about that many years ago, Remington Arms introduced their Accelerator line of saboted center-fire rifle cartridges that allowed shooters to fire light and smaller diameter .223-inch "varmint

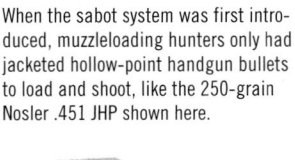

When the sabot system was first introduced, muzzleloading hunters only had jacketed hollow-point handgun bullets to load and shoot, like the 250-grain Nosler .451 JHP shown here.

The selection of plastic sabots offered by Muzzleload Magnum Products allows some bullet diameters to be shot in more than one caliber. Shown here is the 300-grain Speer .451" jacketed flat-nose bullet, with black sabot for use in a .50 caliber and red sabot for use in a .54 caliber bore.

bullets" from larger bore rifles like the .30/30 Winchester or .30/06 Springfield.

During the early 1980s, muzzleloading shooter and hunter Del Ramsey, of Harrison, Arkansas, began his quest for a muzzle-loaded hunting projectile that would deliver better performance on big game than a simple pure-lead round ball or conical bore-sized bullet. He owns a small plastic injection molding company and quickly set out to design a plastic sabot, or cup, which would allow him to load and shoot modern jacketed pistol bullets out of .45, .50 and .54 caliber front-loading rifles. In 1984 he established Muzzleload Magnum Products and since has been the leading manufacturer of muzzleloader sabots. In addition to being marketed under the MMP brand name, Ramsey's sabots are also now sold by a half-dozen or more other companies, which either package the sabots with appropriate hunting bullets or offer the sabots alone for matching up with any appropriate diameter bullet.

The design of the various sabots produced under contract by MMP for other companies, which include Knight Rifles, Hornady Manufacturing, Thompson/Center Arms and Barnes Bullets, may vary slightly from one company to another. However, the basic sabot configuration remains the same. These are a cup-like arrangement, looking very much like the shot cup for a very small-bore shotgun. The "cup" features four petals or sleeves that encompass the cylindrical portion of a bullet, while the base of the sabot features a slightly concave cup with thinner walls that seal the bore when the sabot and bullet are pushed down the barrel by a burning powder charge. The tight grip of the petals or sleeves on the bullet and the rifling of the bore transfer the spin of the rifling to the bullet. At almost the instant the sabot and bullet exit the bore, the petals peel out and away from the bullet and the sabot falls back from the projectile. The bullet is then on its way to the target, without any further influence from the sabot.

Muzzleload Magnum Products currently produces an extensive range of sabots, for rifles ranging in caliber from .36 up to .58. However, the best-selling sabots are those designed to shoot either .44 or .45 caliber bullets from a .50 caliber muzzle-loaded big game rifle. And this shouldn't come as any surprise since modern in-line ignition rifles of .50 caliber currently account for close to 80-percent of all muzzleloaders sold.

Since the introduction of the MMP sabots, one size has remained the best selling—the company's green sabot designed to shoot bullets of .429-430" diameter out of a .50 caliber bore. Ramsey's second best-selling version is a black sabot for loading and shooting .451-.452" projectiles from a fast twist .50 caliber barrel.

He attributes the popularity of the green .50 caliber sabot to the fact that when he first hit the market with his muzzleloader projectile system, there hap-

The all-copper Barnes Expander MZ was the first modern muzzleloader projectile designed expressly for shooting out of a muzzle-loaded rifle with a sabot. The expanded bullet came from a bull elk that went just 50 yards after being hit.

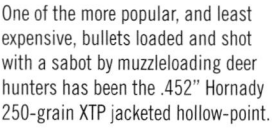

One of the more popular, and least expensive, bullets loaded and shot with a sabot by muzzleloading deer hunters has been the .452" Hornady 250-grain XTP jacketed hollow-point.

pened to be a much greater selection of .429-.430" diameter bullets for the extremely popular .44 Remington Magnum handguns than were available for the venerable ol' .45 handguns. And it was handgun bullets for which the sabots had been designed. However, as a better selection of .451-.452" diameter bullets continue to be developed for powerhouse handguns like the .454 Casull, the popularity of the black .50 caliber sabot has quickly closed on MMP's green .50x.44 sabot.

Experienced in-line .50 caliber muzzleloading rifle shooters have long favored the black .50x.45 sabot over the green .50x.44 sabot for superior accuracy. During the late 1980s, I personally discovered that if I could get one of the early modern in-line ignition muzzleloaders to shoot a 2-inch group at 100 yards with a green MMP sabot and .44 bullet, I could usually get that same rifle to print honest 1½-inch or tighter groups by just switching to the black sabot and a .45 caliber projectile. It became apparent to me and other veteran in-line rifle shooters that the best accuracy tended to come from a bullet and sabot combination that utilized a bullet diameter that was as close to the bore size of the rifle as possible.

When shooting just about any .429-.430" diameter bullet with a green MMP sabot, you'll generally find these laying on the ground 15 to 20 yards from the muzzle of the rifle. However, when shooting with the black sabot and slightly larger diameter .451-.452" bullets, the sabots will normally hit the ground 5 or more yards closer to the muzzle. Early on, my conclusion was that due to the thinner petals or sleeves of the .50x.45 plastic sabots, these tended to peel away from the projectile more rapidly than the thicker and stiffer petals/sleeves of the .50x.44 green sabots. Del Ramsey of Muzzleload Magnum Products agrees.

The tight fit of the sabot in most modern in-line bores helps to seal off the powder charge from damp weather conditions.

Open country such as this often means longer shots. The sabot system generally permits the hunter to load with lighter bullets, for the flattest possible trajectory from a muzzle-loaded big game rifle.

"Had the selection of .45 caliber bullets available today been around in the early 1980s, more than likely I would have never come out with the .44 green sabot," comments Ramsey.

Hornady, Sierra, Nosler, Speer, Barnes, Swift and a few other bullet makers now catalog an unbelievable selection of .44 and .45 caliber bullets, in weights ranging from as light as 180 all the way up to 325 grains. There are a number of bullets in the selection that are ideally suited for loading with a sabot into .50 or .54 caliber rifles for use on any species of big game roaming the North American continent. Unfortunately, there are also a few bullets that were never designed to be shot at the velocities produced by magnum powder charges in a muzzleloading rifle. The construction or design of some bullets simply won't perform well enough for use on big game.

Noted outdoor writer and outdoor television show host Wade Bourne joined me in northern Missouri back in 1987 for his first hunt with a .50 caliber Knight MK-85 in-line rifle and saboted bullets. He was shooting a 100-grain charge of Pyrodex "RS" behind a saboted 180-grain .45 caliber jacketed hollow-point bullet. The load produced a muzzle velocity of about 1,700 f.p.s., with about 1,150 foot-pounds of muzzle energy. The load was extremely accurate, and Wade could easily keep his hits with the scope-sighted muzzleloader inside of 1½ inches at 100 yards.

The second morning of the hunt, he made an easy 40-yard shot on a good eight-point whitetail buck as it slipped past his stand. The deer kicked high into the air, then disappeared over the side of the steep ridge top. Wade waited for most of an hour, then climbed down from his stand and looked for the buck. He followed a good blood trail for more than a quarter mile, then it slowly disappeared. I joined him and we tried picking up the trail, but never found another drop of blood. We returned to where the deer had been standing at the shot to determine the angle of the shot. As Wade climbed back into the stand, I looked down and there laid the entire jacket of the bullet. That light 180-grainer had literally broken apart before ever entering the deer.

Later, I discovered that the bullet had been built for .45 caliber cartridges that produced velocities under 1,000 f.p.s. At about 1,700 f.p.s., the bullet had impacted so hard on such a close target that it did not get the penetration needed to transfer energy to vital internal organs. We never did find that buck.

The 250- and 300-grain .452" diameter Hornady XTP jacketed hollow-point bullets have long been two of my favorite bullets for shooting with a sabot out of a modern in-line muzzleloader. I have shot each of these bullets out of a wide variety of .50 caliber rifles at velocities ranging from around 1,500 f.p.s. all the way up to more than 2,300 f.p.s. In all, I've personally harvested close to 200 big game animals with these two bullets—and I've never had to shoot anything twice!

During one North Carolina muzzleloading deer season a few years ago, I joined a group of nine other veteran muzzleloading hunters to conduct performance tests with the 250- and 300-grain .452" XTP jacketed hollow-point bullets. Everyone in camp was shooting the new Savage Model 10ML II "smokeless powder" muzzleloaders, loading and shooting various loads of Accurate Arms XMP5744, IMR-4227 or VihtaVuori N110. Most of the loads being hunted with pushed a saboted 250-grain XTP out of the muzzle of the 24-inch barrels at around 2,300 f.p.s., and the heftier 300-grain version at around 2,250 f.p.s. These velocities translate into around 2,950 ft. lbs. of energy with the 250-grain loads and right at 3,375 ft. lbs. of knockdown power at the muzzle with the 300-grain Hornady bullet.

In all, our group harvested 42 whitetails during the six-day hunt. These deer were shot at ranges of 40 to 200 yards. A total of 31 deer were taken with the 250-grain bullet, 11 with the heavier 300-grain XTP. Special care was taken to try recovering every bullet that stayed inside these deer, and in the end we did manage to recover 17 of the 250-grain slugs, but only two of the 300-grain bullets were recovered.

Every deer shot went down to single hits. However, it was noted that all but one of the whitetails taken with the 300-grain XTP ran some distance before going down. The average was around 30 yards. On the other hand, most of the deer shot with the lighter 250-grain Hornady bullets practically dropped on the spot. Just four ran any distance after

TOP: For hard to down game, like bear, the muzzleloading hunter can use the same rifle that works well on whitetails, but sighted in with a heavier bullet in the sabot.

BOTTOM: Some of today's more advanced saboted bullet designs bring to the hunter a higher ballistic coefficient for better velocity and energy retention at longer ranges.

Thanks to the versatility of the sabot system, outdoor writer Tom Fegely tailored the load for his .50 caliber Knight MK-85 to permit a "dead on" hold for his shot on this nice pronghorn buck.

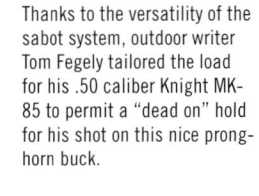

For many younger shooters and women hunters, loads with mild recoil are just as important as the knockdown energy produced by a load. Whitetail hunting fanatic Kandi Kisky used her Knight in-line and saboted bullets to take this great Iowa buck with a low recoiling load.

being hit, and all went less than 20 yards.

From this informal study, the group concluded that the 250-grain XTP jacketed hollow-point proved to be a better choice than the heavier 300-grain version of the same bullet for deer-sized game. Even though, with the powder charges being shot, the heavier bullet produced an average muzzle energy that was more than 400 foot-pounds. greater, the lighter bullet did a better job of putting the deer down cleanly. All of the hunters in camp were experienced muzzleloading hunters, and the general consensus was that the heavier bullet tended to punch on through, taking much of that added energy with it. The lighter 250-grain XTP seemingly did a much better job of transferring most, if not all, of its energy to the target. Nicely expanded 250-grain bullets were recovered from roughly 55 percent of the deer shot with that bullet weight, while less than 20 percent of the deer taken with the 300-grain bullet produced a recovered slug.

During a Nebraska hunt later that same fall, I managed to pull off one of my more memorable muzzleloader shots when I took a nice ten-pointer with the .50 caliber Savage Model 10ML II at 214 yards. For that hunt I was shooting 45 grains of VihtaVuori N110 behind a saboted 250-grain Hornady .45 XTP, loaded with one of the MMP High-Pressure black sabots developed specifically to withstand the higher pressures developed by the smokeless powder loads in the Savage muzzleloader. At the muzzle, this load produces 2,392 f.p.s., with an astounding 3,175 ft. lbs. of energy. Out at the distance I took my buck, the jacketed hollow-point still drove home with nearly 1,200 ft. lbs. of knockdown power. The near 250-pound live-weight whitetail went just 20 feet before going down, and the recovered slug still weighed 246.2 grains.

Before making the switch to the smokeless powder Model 10ML II for most

of my hunting, I hunted often with saboted 260-grain Speer .451" jacketed hollow-point bullets loaded ahead of 90 to 110 grains of Pyrodex "RS/Select." At the muzzle of most in-line percussion hunting rifles with a 22- to 26-inch barrel, this load is good for 1,575 to 1,650 f.p.s., with from around 1,400 to 1,570 ft. lbs. of energy. That bullet was accurate, expanded well and accounted for a lot of deer-sized game for me through the late 1980s and early 1990s. However, when I began to shoot and hunt with magnum 150-grain Pyrodex Pellet charges in a .50 caliber Knight D.I.S.C. Rifle and especially early versions of the Savage smokeless powder muzzleloader, I found it difficult to obtain acceptable accuracy once velocities approached and surpassed 2,000 f.p.s.

During the mid-1990s, several bullet makers began to produce designs specifically for loading and shooting with a plastic sabot out of a muzzleloader. One of the more popular bullets of this type has been the all-copper Expander MZ bullet from Barnes Bullets. The line includes 250- and 300-grain .45 bullets for the .50 caliber rifles and 275- and 325-grain .50 caliber bullets for rifles of .54 caliber. Being all copper, these bullets are significantly longer than jacketed lead-core bullets of similar weight. To ensure proper expansion at downrange velocities of around 1,000 f.p.s., Barnes incorporates a volcanic crater-sized hollow-point opening at the nose.

Out of in-line ignition and other muzzleloading rifles with a rifling twist of one turn-in-24 to 28 inches, the Barnes Expander MZ bullets are generally very accurate and do a great job on game. I've harvested several mature bull elk with the 300-grain version out of .50 caliber rifles, and not one bull went more than 50 yards after being hit. (One of those elk weighed more than 900 pounds on the hoof.) However, this bullet is so long that out of rifles with a turn-in-32 inches or slower rate of twist, they often do not stabilize and keyhole badly. And at higher velocities (1,900+ f.p.s.), the huge opening at the nose seems to hamper accuracy. Anyway, that's been my findings.

Knight Rifles founder Tony Knight took this South Texas whitetail with the very first stainless steel Knight MK-85 and one of his favorite early saboted bullets—the 180-grain .451" Sierra JHP.

During the late 1990s, Knight Rifles contracted with Barnes to produce several all-copper .45 caliber bullets for .50 caliber fast-twist barrels. Marketed as the Knight Red Hot bullets, the lineup includes the standard 250- and 300-grain Expander MZ designs, plus lighter 180-, 200- and 220-grain bullets that feature a dramatically superior aerodynamic hollow-point nose. The resulting better ballistic coefficient of these lighter spire-point all-copper bullets not only improves accuracy at higher muzzleloader velocities, the sharp spire-point frontal shape of these bullets also results in far better retention of velocity and energy down-range.

I've shot the Knight Red Hot bullets out of the .50 caliber Knight D.I.S.C. Rifle and the Thompson/Center Arms break-open Encore 209x50 Magnum models with outstanding accuracy. Loaded with three 50-grain Pyrodex Pellet loads (150-grain powder charges), both of these 26-inch barreled and No. 209 shotshell

When hunting game as small as this Indian black buck antelope, a hunter doesn't need a bullet large enough to bring down a moose. The beauty of the sabot system is that a hunter can match the bullet weight to the game being hunted.

primer ignited muzzleloaders are capable of getting a 220-grain "Red Hot" bullet out of the muzzle at close to 2,200 f.p.s. with around 2,400 ft. lbs. of energy. At 100 yards, each of these rifles can print the sharp-nosed hollow-point bullet inside of 1½ inches. And at that distance the all-copper bullet would still be capable of delivering more then 1,600 ft. lbs. of energy. All the way out at 200 yards, the bullet would still hit with more than 1,100 ft. lbs. of punch.

When stoked up with a 44.5-grain charge of VihtaVuori N110 smokeless powder, the .50 caliber Savage Model 10ML II spits the saboted 220-grain Knight Red Hot bullet out of the muzzle at 2,435 f.p.s. and generates 2,893 ft. lbs. of energy. Thanks to the improved aerodynamics of this bullet, it does maintain velocity better downrange, which also means it retains higher energy levels out at 100 and 200 yards better than bullets with a large hollow point or flat frontal surface. In fact, when fired from the Model 10ML II at just over 2,400 f.p.s., the 220-grain "Red Hot" bullet hits with around 1,900 ft. lbs. of energy at 100 yards and continues to drive home with about 1,400 ft. lbs. of knockdown power out at 200 yards.

Until just the past few years, muzzleloading hunters pretty well had been faced with loading and shooting only pistol bullets with a sabot in the fast rifling twist bore of their favorite muzzle-loaded big game rifles. While many of the bullets available have proven far superior as hunting projectiles to the soft lead round ball and heavy lead bore-sized conical bullets, these bullets lack the aerodynamics to adequately maintain needed velocities and energy levels at the outer limits of a big game muzzleloader's maximum effective range. Knight Rifles, Thompson/Center Arms, Connecticut Valley Arms, Traditions, and now Savage Arms have all established that their rifles are still lethal on larger game at 200 yards and slightly farther. However, some of the bullets we've been shooting may not be.

The 250-grain Hornady .452" XTP has been a stellar performer for me out of a number of modern in-line rifles, and I've taken deer with it all the way out past 200 yards. This bullet has a ballistic coefficient of .147. Loaded with an MMP sabot and a 150-grain charge of Pyrodex Pellets, a 26-inch barreled No. 209 primer ignited rifle like the Encore 209x50 Magnum from Thompson/Center Arms will produce a muzzle velocity of right at 2,000 f.p.s. Due to the poor ballistic coefficient of this bullet, it slows to 1,525 f.p.s. at 100 yards and is all the way down to 1,170 f.p.s. when it reaches 200 yards. At the muzzle, the load is good for 2,220 ft. lbs. of energy...at 100 yards it hits with 1,287 ft. lbs....and retains just 760 ft. lbs. of energy by the time it gets to 200 yards.

For comparison, let's look at the downrange ballistics of the 220-grain Knight "Red Hot" bullet. A 100-grain charge of Hodgdon Triple Seven black powder substitute will push this bullet from the muzzle of a 26-inch .50 caliber Knight barrel at just over 2,000 f.p.s. This bullet has a ballistic coefficient of .217. The considerably better ballistic coefficient of this bullet design allows it to still be speeding along at about 1,660 f.p.s. at 100 yards and about 1,375 f.p.s. at 200 yards. Because this bullet is 30 grains lighter than the 250-grain XTP, it produces a muzzle energy of 1,954 ft. lbs., or about 275 ft. lbs. less energy at the muzzle when shot from the barrel at 2,000 f.p.s. However, thanks to the better aerodynamics, the lighter 220-grain "Red Hot" delivers greater energy levels downrange. At 100 yards, the bullet would still have close to 1,350 ft. lbs. of punch and at 200 yards it would still hit a whitetail with around 925 ft. lbs. of energy.

Now that we have muzzleloading big game rifles capable of getting a saboted bullet out of the muzzle at velocities exceeding 2,000 f.p.s., a few bullet makers are now stepping up to the plate with better bullet designs for improved downrange performance on big game. Here's a look at a few of the more recent bullet designs.

Parker Productions, a relatively new and small custom bullet making operation located in Moscow, Idaho, is now producing a jacketed version of the so-called Hydra-Con muzzleloader hunting bullets they have been offering since the mid-1990s. These were originally available only as a "bore-sized" bullet to be loaded without a sabot. But due to the fast-growing popularity of shooting saboted bullets, the company began offering swaged lead Hydra-Con bullets in .45 caliber in the late 1990s. These have been used very successfully with sabots by a number of muzzleloading big game hunters to harvest everything from deer to moose.

What makes this muzzleloader projectile unique is its internal design. Hidden inside is a hollow cavity, which is capped with a soft lead tip. Beneath this cap, sitting directly on top of the internal cavity is a tiny steel ball that's slightly larger in diameter than the cavity. When this bullet hits, the lead cap pushes rearward, forcing the steel ball into the hollow cavity. The result is tremendous expansion.

One problem encountered when shooting a pure lead bullet in a sabot at velocities exceeding 2,000 f.p.s. can be that the bullet simply won't stand up to the hard push of magnum powder charges, and accuracy can really suffer. This is especially true when shooting the smokeless powder loads used in a Savage Model 10ML II. Not only does the soft lead overobturate (or flatten in the sabot) at the moment of ignition, a soft lead bullet will also tend to bell out at the base. This puts most of the outward pressure against the sabot sleeves where they attach to the base. By the time the bullet exits the muzzle, the tremendous amount of friction produced where the lead bullet bells out causes the sabot sleeve to wear completely through. Bullet, sabot base and sleeves often exit the muzzle separate from one another.

Dwain Parker of Parker Productions has remedied the problem by completely redesigning the Hydra-Con bullet for today's sabot-shooting high performance muzzleloading big game rifles. The new design is constructed with a copper jacket and a more aerodynamic nose. In fact, the 250-grain jacketed Hydra-Con bullet has a ballistic coefficient of right at .230, while the heavier 300-grain version offers a b.c. of close to .290. Shot with three 50-grain Pyrodex Pellets

Two of today's more popular polymer-tipped spire-point bullet designs for loading with a sabot into a muzzle-loaded big game rifle are shown here—the Precision Rifle "QT" bullet (left) and the Hornady SST (right).

Precision Rifle offers muzzle-loading hunters one of the more unique bullet concepts with their "duplex" sabot-within-a-sabot "Dead Center" arrangement that allows a long cylindrical (and high b.c.) .357 diameter bullet to be loaded into and shot from a .50 caliber bore.

out of a Thompson/Center Arms in-line ignition rifle with a 26-inch barrel, the 250-grain Parker bullet would exit the muzzle at the same 2,000 f.p.s. achieved with the Hornady XTP of the same weight. At the muzzle, energy levels would be the same as well. However, the considerably higher ballistic coefficient of this bullet would result in nearly 300 ft. lbs. of additional energy at 100 yards than possible with the .452" Hornady pistol bullet. At 200 yards, the bullet would have about 330 ft. lbs. of added game taking energy.

Another new muzzleloading bullet design that's taking this old sport into the future is the sleek SST from Hornady Manufacturing. Here is another sharp-nosed spire-point with dramatically improved aerodynamics and a high ballistic coefficient for greater retention of velocity and energy out past 200 yards. As this book was written, Hornady was offering .452" SST bullets in two weights—250- and 300-grain. The company also produces a 200-grain .400" SST for shooting with a sabot out of a .45 caliber rifle. (The company has shared that they have a 180-grain .400" SST planned if the .45 caliber muzzleloading big game rifles continue to grow in popularity.)

The SST is a serious high performance muzzleloading hunting projectile that incorporates many of the features Hornady builds into their similar line of center-fire rifle bullets. These include a tapered thickness jacket that's considerably heavier at the base, thinning toward the tip. The bullet features a sharp polymer tip sitting into a shallow hollow cavity. Upon impact, the tip pushes rearward to promote full expansion of the SST.

And to keep this bullet from fragmenting or coming apart, Hornady incorporates its internal "Inter-Lock" ring which eliminates overexpansion.

The ballistic coefficient of the 250-grain SST is right at .240, while the 300-grain .452" bullet has a b.c. of around .290. The 200-grainer for the .45 caliber bore sports a b.c. of .225. What these numbers mean to the modern-day muzzle-loading hunter is greatly improved downrange performance on game. With some of the hotter loads shot out of today's ultra modern in-line rifles, the higher ballistic coefficient of the SST design will mean upward of 30 percent MORE knockdown power than possible with a hollow-point pistol bullet of the same weight shot at the same muzzle velocity.

Still another new saboted muzzle-loaded hunting projectile design is the "Dead Center" bullet from Precision Rifle of Manitoba, Canada. The bullets from this maker are non-jacketed cold swaged pure lead bullets, also tipped with a sharp polymer (plastic) tip. What sets the Precision Rifle bullets apart from practically all other saboted muzzleloader bullets are the extremely high ballistic coefficients of these bullets. The saboted .45 caliber "Dead Center" bullet (for shooting in either a .50 or .54 fast-twist bore) has a b.c. of .376, and as far as I know, that's the highest ballistic coefficient of any bullet for a .50 caliber muzzleloader.

Perhaps the most unique offering from Precision Rifle is the sleek 175- and 195-grain .357" diameter bullets designed to be loaded into and shot from a .50 caliber bore. In order to load such a small diameter projectile into such a large bore requires a novel approach with the sabot, or rather sabots. To load the .357" bullet into a .500" bore requires loading the bullet in a special flat-based .45x.357 sabot, which is then placed in a .50x.45 sabot. Some shooters are reporting exceptional accuracy with this "sabot-within-a-sabot" concept. Del Ramsey, of Muzzle-load Magnum Products, supplies the sabots for the Precision Rifle bullets and took one of his best ever whitetails with the 175-grain .357" diameter "Dead Center" bullet. He was using 120 grains of GOEX ClearShot behind the bullet, and out of the 28-inch barrel of his .50 caliber Thompson/Center Omega, the load is good for 2,000 f.p.s. and produces consistent 1" groups for Ramsey. He shot the huge-bodied buck at about 80 yards. The deer went less than 10 yards.

Back in 1985, when Tony Knight introduced his first MK-85 in-line rifle, saboted bullets were illegal to use in more than a dozen states. Today, only a couple of states do not allow them to be used during the muzzleloader seasons. In fact, more whitetails are now harvested with saboted bullets than with all other types of muzzleloader projectiles combined. In the following chapters, this book will share tips on achieving the best accuracy with these and other muzzleloading projectiles, plus will compare the downrange energy of older and newer bullet designs, along with helpful pointers for coping with muzzleloader trajectories.

WARNING: **The smokeless powder loads given for the Savage Model 10ML II should only be used in that rifle. Currently it is the only muzzleloader manufactured for use with specific smokeless powders. Unless the maker of your muzzleloader prescribes the use of smokeless powder, it's still muzzleloading as usual— load and shoot only black powder or an approved black powder substitute.**

choosing
A POWDER

FAR RIGHT: The goal of every
big game hunter is to make a
clean, quick humane shot. Choosing the right propellant plays a
big role in getting optimum
performance from your modern
muzzleloading hunting rifle.

BELOW: Black powder, such
as the GOEX brand (below), is
a "Class A Explosive," while
Pyrodex (below right) has been
classified as a "Flammable Solid."

The basic ingredients for black powder has remained unchanged since the first muzzle-loaded firearms appeared on the battlefield nearly 700 years ago. No one individual can be credited with the actual invention of black powder, nor can one location be credited with being the birthplace of the explosive propellant. So, the origins of this concoction of sulfur, charcoal and saltpeter (potassium nitrate) to this day remain something of a mystery.

Through the years, various manufacturers varied the amounts or percentages of the basic ingredients used, mixed those ingredients in different ways, used different wetting agents to combine the ingredients into one, and often mixed in a few other things in attempts to improve the performance of black powder. And performance is what has appealed to the individual pulling the trigger far more than what's in that charge of powder. In that regard, today's shooter expects far more out of the load in his or her muzzle-loaded big game rifle than any shooter of the past, and for that reason the vast majority of today's shooters no longer load and shoot the propellant that was the mainstay of this shooting sport for some seven centuries. Following is a look at the various different powders that are now used in rifles of front-loading design. We will also discuss the benefits of each powder as well as any negative characteristics of a particular muzzleloading propellant. This chapter will also look at basic loads with each type of powder.

Black Powder

Black powder for use in sporting muzzle-loaded firearms is currently being imported from several foreign countries. However, the one U.S. manufacturer that currently supplies the majority of the ancient propellant that's still being used by as few as 10 percent of all muzzleloading shooters in this country today is GOEX, Inc. (formerly known as Gearhart-Owen Explosives), now located in Doyline, Louisiana.

While the process of making the powder has remained basically the same for hundreds of years, much of the equipment used by the new GOEX plant is far more advanced. The company has also established quality control procedures that help ensure the purity and quality of the ingredients that go into each and every

batch of powder. Likewise, improved sifting and screening processes make the powder now being produced by GOEX very likely the most consistent black powder ever produced at any time, anywhere in the world. And like powder of this type produced some 200 years ago in this country, GOEX still relies on the *"F"* grading of the powder that muzzleloading shooters have accepted since it was adopted by the E. Irene du Pont black powder plant during the early 1800s. (It should be noted that the first powder mill established in the American colonies was built near Milton, Massachusetts in 1675. By 1800, there were more than 200 black powder plants operating in the newly formed United States.)

As many as seven or eight grades, or granulations, of sporting black powder have been available at one time or another. However, four basic grades have stood the test of time as the most widely used—Fg, FFg, FFFg and FFFFg. The more "Fs" that appear in the granulaiton, the finer the grains. And the finer the grains are, the more explosive the granulation becomes.

Fg is the coarsest and slowest burning of the black powder grades. This granulation is generally considered musket powder, for use in big smoothbores like the .69 caliber Charleville and .75 caliber Brown Bess muskets dating from the Revolutionary War. FFg is pretty well accepted as rifle powder, for use in muzzle-loaded rifles of .50 and .54 caliber (as well as the .45 caliber with big heavy lead conical bullets). FFFg is the granulation best suited for the small chambers of percussion revolvers, short-barreled single-shot muzzle-loaded handguns and small-bore muzzleloading small game rifles of .32 to .40 caliber (and often round ball loads in a .45 or even .50 caliber rifle). FFFFg is the dust-like granulation that is very explosive and easy to ignite and is used for priming the pan of a flintlock ignition system.

We could spend a lot more time here discussing black powder, but since so few still load and shoot the propellant, we'll just jump into the benefits and the negatives of shooting this powder. First a look at the downside of shooting black powder.

Hard To Find—Just finding a dealer who will handle black powder becomes increasingly more difficult. Since the powder has been officially classified as a "Class A Explosive," as you can expect, there is often a lot of red tape involved with shipping, storage, sale, transportation and, in a few specific locations, even the possession of the explosive. For that reason, few dealers want the added headache of offering the powder.

Modern in-line rifles like this Knight D.I.S.C. Rifle can get a light saboted projectile out of the muzzle at well over 2,000 f.p.s. when loaded with one of today's better performing black powder substitutes.

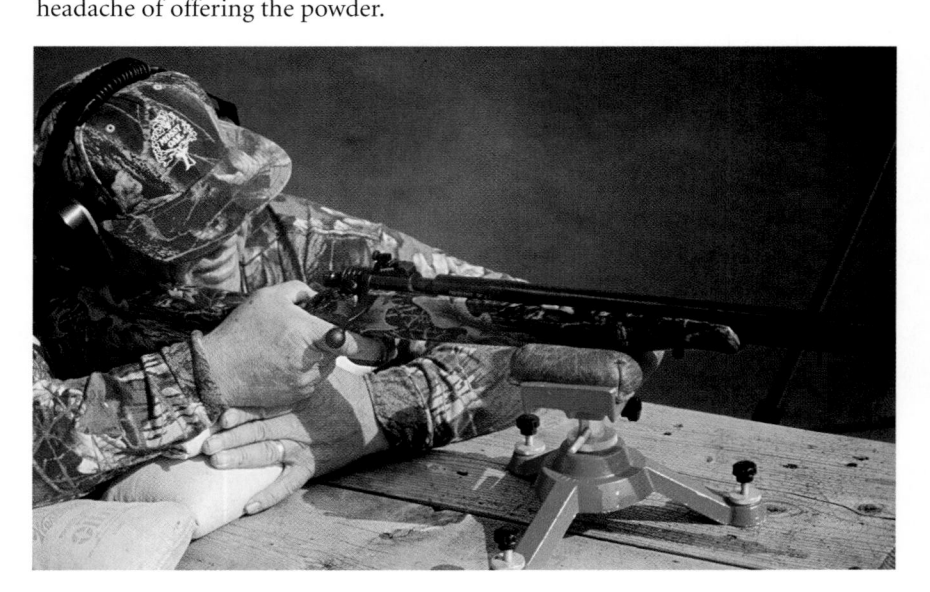

Fouls Badly—Anyone who has shot black powder loads will attest to how dirty this powder burns. One shot will leave enough fouling in the rifling to make it impossible to even think about trying to push a second plastic sabot and bullet down the bore. And of all the different muzzleloading powders, black powder leaves behind the most corrosive residue. This fouling will literally pull moisture right out of the air, and during extremely humid conditions can begin to destroy a bore (and any other metal surface coated with the fouling) in a matter of hours. The fouling also continues to build with each succeeding shot.

Now…The plus side of shooting black powder loads.

Shoots Best in Some Rifles—Many bore-sized conical bullet shooters have continued to use FFg in their rifles instead of switching to a modern black powder substitute like Pyrodex or Triple Seven. With some of the big bullets and in some rifles, this old mixture of charcoal, sulfur and potassium nitrate simply performs best. Likewise, when a small-bore shooter is looking to get a .32 or .36 caliber "squirrel rifle" to print those tiny sphere's of lead accurate enough to permit head shots on bushytails or cottontails, FFFg very often will get the job done while the finer grades of a substitute may not produce the desired accuracy.

Long Storage Life—As long as black powder is stored in a cool, dry place, the powder is good for years. Many shooters have shot black powder that was 10…20…30 or more years old, and the powder still performed as well as powder from a can produced a year ago. This is even true of black powder that had been opened and resealed.

TYPICAL BLACK POWDER LOADS > 24- TO 28-INCH BARREL

	BULLET	CHARGE	MUZZLE VELOCITY	MUZZLE ENERGY
.45 RIFLE	128 gr. .440"RB	70 gr. FFFg	1,950 f.p.s.	1,080 f.p.e.
	240 gr. T/C "Maxi-Ball"	90 gr. FFg	1,659 f.p.s.	1,466 f.p.e.
	158 gr. .357"/MMP Sabot	80 gr. FFg	1,840 f.p.s.	1,186 f.p.e.
.50 RIFLE	178 gr. .490"RB	90 gr. FFg	1,950 f.p.s.	1,502 f.p.e.
	370 gr. T/C "Maxi-Ball"	100 gr. FFg	1,418 f.p.s.	1,648 f.p.e.
	250 gr. Hornady .452" XTP/MMP Sabot	100 gr. FFg	1,625 f.p.s.	1,462 f.p.e.
.54 RIFLE	230 gr. .530"RB	100 gr. FFg	1,855 f.p.s.	1,758 f.p.e.
	430 gr. T/C "Maxi-Ball"	110 gr. FFg	1,428 f.p.s.	1,948 f.p.e.
	300 gr. Hornady .452" XTP/MMP Sabot	110 gr. FFg	1,578 f.p.s.	1,656 f.p.e.

Pyrodex

Introduced during the mid-1970s, Pyrodex became the first truly successful black powder substitute. Unlike black powder, which has always been classified as an explosive, Pyrodex has been officially classified as a "flammable solid," the same as modern nitrocellulose-based smokeless powders. However, the Hodgdon Powder Company-produced propellant contains little of the ingredients used to produce smokeless powder, or the extremely high pressures created by smokeless powder loads that can completely destroy all but one modern muzzleloading rifle —the Savage Model 10ML II. (See Chapter 5, "The Birth of Smokeless Muzzleloading.")

Thanks to the relaxed classification on this powder, which contains all of the ingredients used to make black powder, Pyrodex has far fewer restrictions imposed upon it. In fact, this powder can be placed right on dealers' shelves, just like boxes of shotgun shells. And with less restrictive shipping regulations, by the end of the 1980s Pyrodex had already replaced black powder as the most widely shot muzzleloader propellant in North America. The powder can be easily found in most gun shops and large sporting goods stores. In fact, today's muzzleloading hunter can walk right into most stores of a mass merchandiser like Wal-Mart and pick up a pound of Pyrodex.

Like the black powder it replaces, Pyrodex comes in several different grades or granulations. The three that should be of the only interest to today's performance-minded muzzleloading hunter are "P," "RS" and "Select." The "P" Grade of Pyrodex is basically the equivalent of FFFg black powder, for use in percussion revolvers. The fine grain and faster burning rate of this powder also makes it an excellent choice for use in some small-bore small-game rifles, while a few .45 and .50 caliber in-line shooters often use the granulation to achieve higher velocities and energy levels with saboted bullets. Pyrodex in

Just a single shot with either black powder or Pyrodex can leave enough fouling in the bore to turn a white cotton cleaning patch nearly black. This fouling can adversely affect accuracy.

"RS" Grade is the close equivalent of FFg black powder, formulated for use in larger bore muzzleloading rifles and shotguns. And "Select" is a more uniform Match Grade of "RS" for those shooters who seek optimum accuracy from the rifle and bullet they shoot.

Wherever a shooter can find both black powder and Pyrodex for sale, chances are the latter will retail for a couple of dollars more. However, Pyrodex is bulkier than black powder, giving you approximately 30 percent more volume of powder per pound. A shooter should load any of the Pyrodex grades or granulations on a "volume equivalent" basis to loads of black powder. Hodgdon recommends using the very same volumetric powder measures used to load black powder. Pyrodex has been formulated to give basically the same performance that's produced by the same volume of black powder. In other words, if you load and shoot 100 grains of FFg black powder, the same powder measure at the same setting will give you the same basic ballistics. However, by actual weight, the Pyrodex charge will weigh, on a balance beam or electronic powder scale, just 70 grains. If you weigh all of your powder charges, always remember to weigh Pyrodex loads 30 percent lighter than the black powder loads for the same rifle and bullet.

Another Benefit—In addition to giving a shooter more shots per pound, Pyrodex will allow, to some degree, successive shots without having to wipe the bore. This is especially true when shooting some of the bore-sized conical bullets that have been lubed with an advanced bullet grease that helps keep the fouling soft. While the fouling that is left behind does not tend to build as rapidly as black powder fouling, after three or four shots, the sabot shooter can find it extremely difficult to push another plastic sabot down the bore. And with each succeeding shot, accuracy will really begin to open up. However, for those emergency situations when you need a quick follow-up shot (or two) to finish off a down but not quite out big game animal, Pyrodex fouling won't hamper you that much.

Loading Pyrodex—Pyrodex is harder to ignite than black powder, so if your rifle uses No. 11 caps for ignition, always rely on the hottest caps you can find. In some side-hammer percussion ignition systems, and especially in a rifle of flintlock design, drop in a light 5-grain charge of FFFg or FFFFg first, then the Pyrodex charge. This will give 100 percent ignition every time. If your rifle utilizes a hotter musket cap or No. 209 primer for ignition, never worry about ignition with any of the Pyrodex powders. Just be sure to put a bit of compression on the powder charge when seating the projectile. Pyrodex tends to ignite best and to give more uniform velocities when compacted by 25 to 40 pounds of pressure on the ramrod. And use the same amount of pressure every time. The reward will be better accuracy.

Poor Shelf Life—Very likely the biggest drawback to working up loads with Pyrodex is the relatively short shelf life of the powder. Once a can has been opened and the factory seal broken, that can of propellant should be completely used within three to four months in order to benefit from its full power. A partial can that is held onto for any length of time will begin to give erratic performance, and getting the same top-end velocities that were achieved from a freshly opened can becomes impossible. If you've ever tried to keep a half or a third of a canister from one season to the next, I'm probably not telling you anything you haven't already experienced. A modern in-line rifle that can consistently punch 1½-inch, 100-yard groups with fresh powder will generally do good to keep hits inside of 4 to 5 inches when loaded with Pyrodex that has been open for six to nine months, or longer.

TYPICAL PYRODEX LOADS > 24- TO 28-INCH BARREL

	BULLET	CHARGE	MUZZLE VELOCITY	MUZZLE ENERGY
.45 RIFLE	150 gr. .400" Knight "Red Hot" with High Pressure Sabot	80 gr. "RS/Sel"	1,920 f.p.s.	1,227 f.p.e.
	200 gr. .400" Hornady SST/Hornady Sabot	100 gr. "P"	2,075 f.p.s.	1,910 f.p.e.
	285 gr. Buffalo Bullet HP/HB Conical	100 gr. "RS/Sel"	1,458 f.p.s.	1,339 f.p.e.
.50 RIFLE	200 gr. Knight .451" "Red Hot"/MMP Sabot	100 gr. "RS/Sel"	1,810 f.p.s.	1,454 f.p.e.
	200 gr. Knight .451" "Red Hot"/MMP Sabot	100 gr. "P"	1,954 f.p.s.	1,700 f.p.e.
	240 gr. .429" Hornady XTP/MMP Sabot	100 gr. "RS/Sel"	1,655 f.p.s.	1,560 f.p.e.
	250 gr. .452" Hornady SST/Hornady Sabot	100 gr. "P"	1,730 f.p.s.	1,660 f.p.e.
	300 gr. .452" Hornady SST/Hornady Sabot	110 gr. "RS/Sel"	1,610 f.p.s.	1,725 f.p.e.
	370 gr. T/C "Maxi-Ball"	100 gr. "RS/Sel"	1,525 f.p.s.	1,905 f.p.e.
.54 RIFLE	260 gr. Speer .451" JHP/MMP Sabot	100 gr. "RS/Sel"	1,620 f.p.s.	1,513 f.p.e.
	300 gr. .452" Hornady XTP/MMP Sabot	110 gr. "RS/Sel"	1,595 f.p.s.	1,695 f.p.e.
	425 gr. Buffalo Bullet HP/HB Conical	120 gr. "RS/Sel"	1,536 f.p.s.	2,222 f.p.e.

Pyrodex Pellets

Convenience has its price—and when a shooter turns to the very convenient compressed Pyrodex Pellets to eliminate the need for measuring out a charge of loose-grain powder (or the need for a powder measure for that matter), the actual cost per shot skyrockets dramatically! As this chapter was being written, a box of a hundred 50-grain (black powder equivalent) pellets carried an average retail price of about $26. When weighed, a shooter will find that these 50-grain pellets actually weigh just round 38 grains. Well, a pound (Avoirdupois) is 7,000 grains, which means that a box of 100 of the 50-grain equivalent pellets actually weighs only slightly more than a half-pound. That takes the convenience cost of shooting pellets to around $50 per pound. If you shoot 100-grain (2-pellet) loads and shoot an average of 100 shots per year, you'll spend right at $50 for powder (2 boxes). If you shoot the heavy 150-grain charges, the cost for 100 shots will jump to around $75 (3 boxes of pellets).

There is no denying the convenience of simply dropping in two or three of the pellets, then seating the bullet over the charge. One end of each pellet features a darker coating that is a more sensitive igniter. When loading the pellets, this end is always dropped in first. Since the powder is already in a compressed state, there is actually no need to put any more pressure on the ramrod than needed to get the projectile over the powder. In fact, if excessive pressure is used, a shooter can crumble the pellets, changing the burning characteristics of the powder, and this will commonly show up on the target as a flier or an erratic group.

Both of these charges are 100-grain Pyrodex equivalents to that volume of black powder. However, the compressed pellets on the right will cost you two to four times as much to shoot.

TYPICAL PYRODEX PELLET LOADS > 24- TO 28-INCH BARREL

	BULLET	CHARGE	MUZZLE VELOCITY	MUZZLE ENERGY
.45 RIFLE	150 gr. Knight .400" "Red Hot"/ Brown High Pressure Sabot	100 gr. (2) 50 gr./.45 cal.	2,225 f.p.s.	1,650 f.p.e.
	150 gr. Knight .400" "Red Hot"/ Brown High Pressure Sabot	150 gr. (3) 50 gr./.45 cal.	2,470 f.p.s.	2,032 f.p.e.
	200 gr. Hornady .400" SST/Knight HP Sabot	100 gr. (2) 50 gr./.45 cal.	1,945 f.p.s.	1,680 f.p.e.
	200 gr. Hornady .400" SST/Knight HP Sabot	150 gr. (3) 50 gr./.45 cal.	2,247 f.p.s.	2,240 f.p.e.
	225 gr. Power Belt Conical	100 gr. (2) 50 gr./.45 cal.	1,795 f.p.s.	1,608 f.p.e.
.50 RIFLE	240 gr. .429" Hornady XTP/MMP Sabot	100 gr. (2) 50 gr./.50 cal.	1,730 f.p.s.	1,593 f.p.e.
	250 gr. .452" Hornady SST/Hornady Sabot	100 gr. (2) 50 gr./.50 cal.	1,705 f.p.s.	1,612 f.p.e.
	250 gr. .452" Hornady SST/Hornady Sabot	150 gr. (3) 50 gr./.50 cal.	1,975 f.p.s.	2,162 f.p.e.
	300 gr. .452" Hornady SST/Hornady Sabot	150 gr. (3) 50 gr./.50 cal.	1,910 f.p.s.	2,430 f.p.e.
	350 gr. T/C "Maxi-Hunter" Conical	100 gr. (2) 50 gr./.50 cal.	1,518 f.p.s.	1,792 f.p.e.
.54 RIFLE	300 gr. .452" Hornady XTP/MMP Sabot	120 gr. (2) 60 gr./.54 cal.	1,701 f.p.s.	1,923 f.p.e.
	325 gr. .500" Speer JHP/MMP Sabot	120 gr. (2) 60 gr./.54 cal.	1,645 f.p.s.	1,950 f.p.e.
	430 gr. White PowerPunch Conical	120 gr. (2) 60 gr./.54 cal.	1,425 f.p.s.	1,935 f.p.e.

Hodgdon Powder Company presently offers Pyrodex Pellets in diameters specifically for .45, .50 and .54 caliber rifles. For .45 and .50, these are offered in 50- and 30-grain (black powder equivalent) charges. In .54, the pellets are offered in just 60-grain size. While the majority of today's modern in-line rifle manufacturers heavily promote the use of magnum 150-grain pellet charges, Hodgdon has established a 120-grain pellet charge as the maximum charge they recommend.

Triple Seven—FFg, FFFg and Pellets

Introduced in 2002, Hodgdon's Triple Seven has to be the finest black powder substitute to date. It's certainly the cleanest burning safe alternative we have ever had. And part of the reason why this new powder does burn so much cleaner is that the formulation does not include sulfur, which is the ingredient found in both black powder and Pyrodex that is so darn corrosive. However, Hodgdon does not claim that Triple Seven is noncorrosive. But they do claim that the fouling left behind by the burning powder can be thoroughly cleaned from the bore and other metal surfaces with nothing more than water.

When this was written, the company was offering their latest muzzleloader propellant in FFg and FFFg loose-grain granulation, and in 50-grain compressed pellets. The latter does not actually weigh 50 grains, but is the equivalent of 50 grains of black powder. By actual weight, the pellets checked averaged right at 30 grains. And considering that at an average retail of $30 per box of 100, a pound (7,000 grains) of Triple Seven will cost you more than $70!

That's the bad news. The good news is that Triple Seven loose-grain powder is actually hotter than the pellets. And that's because Hodgdon formulated the pellets to produce basically the same ballistics (and pressures) of Pyrodex Pellets. The company does not recommend the use of 150-grain pellet loads. However, as already pointed out, a number of high performance muzzleloading big game rifle makers have long been promoting the use of those magnum charges of Pyrodex Pellets. And Hodgdon knew that shooters would immediately try loading with three Triple Seven pellets as well. So, a 150-grain Triple Seven Pellet load is not as hot as a 150-grain FFFg Triple Seven load. And that's not by accident.

The muzzleloading hunter looking for the absolute maximum knockdown power he can get from his modern bullet-shooting (sabot or bore-sized conical) rifle can practically duplicate the ballistics of a three 50-grain Triple Seven load by loading just 100 grains of FFFg Triple Seven. (Take a look at the accompanying load tables.) And a pound of loose-grain Triple Seven (in either FFg or FFFg) typically retailed for $22 to $24 at this writing.

Adam Bridges—the author's son—used a modern in-line rifle to take this fine buck. These rifles produce top velocities with hefty loads of Hodgdon's new Triple Seven black powder substitute. A 100-grain charge of FFFg Triple Seven is nearly the equivalent to 150-grain charges of Pyrodex "P."

TYPICAL TRIPLE SEVEN LOADS (Loose) > 24- TO 28-INCH BARREL

	BULLET	CHARGE	MUZZLE VELOCITY	MUZZLE ENERGY
.45 RIFLE	180 gr. Hornady .400" XTP/MMP Sabot	100 gr. FFg	2,108 f.p.s.	1,778 f.p.e.
	180 gr. Hornady .400" XTP/MMP Sabot	100 gr. FFFg	2,225 f.p.s.	1,980 f.p.e.
	225 gr. Power Belt Conical	90 gr. FFg	1,784 f.p.s.	1,586 f.p.e.
	225 gr. Power Belt Conical	90 gr. FFFg	1,799 f.p.s.	1,617 f.p.e.
.50 RIFLE	240 gr. Hornady .452" XTP/MMP Sabot	100 gr. FFg	1,820 f.p.s.	1,764 f.p.e.
	240 gr. Hornady .452" XTP/MMP Sabot	100 gr. FFFg	1,941 f.p.s.	2,004 f.p.e.
	300 gr. Hornady .452" SST/Hornady Sabot	100 gr. FFg	1,778 f.p.s.	2,100 f.p.e.
	300 gr. Hornady .452" SST/Hornady Sabot	100 gr. FFFg	1,847 f.p.s.	2,265 f.p.e.
	410 gr. Hornady Great Plains Conical w/wad	100 gr. FFg	1,508 f.p.s.	2,070 f.p.e.
	410 gr. Hornady Great Plains Conical w/wad	100 gr. FFFg	1,594 f.p.s.	2,316 f.p.e.
.54 RIFLE	250 gr. Nosler "Shots"/Harvester Sabot	100 gr. FFg	1,789 f.p.s.	1,775 f.p.e.
	250 gr. Nosler "Shots"/Harvester Sabot	100 gr. FFFg	1,892 f.p.s.	1,987 f.p.e.
	425 gr. Hornady Great Plains Conical	100 gr. FFg	1,499 f.p.s.	2,125 f.p.e.

TYPICAL TRIPLE SEVEN PELLET LOADS > 24- TO 28-INCH BARREL

	BULLET	CHARGE	MUZZLE VELOCITY	MUZZLE ENERGY
.45 RIFLE	200 gr. Hornady .400" SST/Hornady Sabot	100 gr. (2) 50 gr./.45 cal.	1,958 f.p.s.	1,700 f.p.e.
	200 gr. Hornady .400" SST/Hornady Sabot	150 gr. (3) 50 gr./.45 cal.	2,262 f.p.s.	2,270 f.p.e.
.50 RIFLE	250 gr. Hornady .452" SST/Hornady Sabot	100 gr. (2) 50 gr./.50 cal.	1,765 f.p.s.	1,725 f.p.e.
	250 gr. Hornady .452" SST/Hornady Sabot	150 gr. (3) 50 gr./.50 cal.	2,069 f.p.s.	2,375 f.p.e.
	300 gr. Hornady .452" SST/Hornady Sabot	100 gr. (2) 50 gr./.50 cal.	1,680 f.p.s.	1,878 f.p.e.
	300 gr. Hornady .452" SST/Hornady Sabot	150 gr. (3) 50 gr./.50 cal.	1,936 f.p.s.	2,490 f.p.e.

Other Black Powder Substitutes

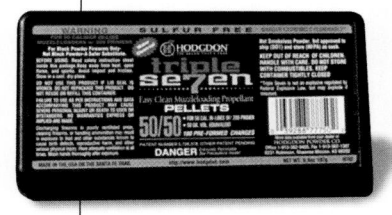

Triple Seven Pellets make loading easier and quicker, eliminating the need to precisely measure a charge of loose-grain powder.

Since the early 1980s, several other black powder substitutes have come and gone. Names like Golden Powder, Black Canyon Powder, Black Mag and a few others are hardly remembered by today's muzzleloading shooters. More recently, GOEX introduced another powder known as Clear Shot, which, too, contained no sulfur. Many shooters reported excellent accuracy with the propellant; however, recorded velocities were considerably slower than those with an equal amount of Pyrodex behind the same projectile. GOEX had stopped production of the powder about the time this book was being written. Muzzleloading has become a very performance-driven hunting sport, and today's shooter wants both exceptional accuracy and top velocity. Hopefully, the company will find a way to give the powder the "oomph!" needed to compete with Triple Seven and reintroduce it in the near future. It's always good to have choices.

American Pioneer Powder (Boca Raton, Florida) is currently producing another black powder substitute that's being marketed under the same name. This is actually the continued production of another powder, just under a new name. Some of you may be familiar with a powder sold as Clean Shot. This is the same muzzleloader propellant, just slightly more refined.

During the winter/spring of 2001, I did quite a bit of shooting with "Clean Shot" and actually found the loose-grain FFg and FFFg powder to perform every bit as good as Pyrodex. At that time, the company also marketed pellets that were extremely similar to Pyrodex Pellets, complete with the small hole through the center which promoted a more complete burn of magnum charges. In fact, the design was "too close" and Hodgdon took legal action to have the production of the Clean Shot Pellets discontinued. Under the new name, American Pioneer Powder is offering FFg and FFFg black powder substitute, plus a newly designed "pellet" that's somewhat rectangular in shape—and without a hole through the center.

Smokeless Loads for the Savage Model 10ML II

Ever since William "Tony" Knight first introduced the Knight MK-85 in-line percussion rifle to the growing ranks of muzzleloading hunters, they have constantly tried to get these modern-looking rifles to shoot as hard and with the same accuracy as many modern center-fire big game rifles. Through the 1990s and into the first few years of the 21st Century, the evolution of the high performance muzzleloading big game rifle has been in high gear. And just a glance at the ballistics given in this chapter will confirm that some of the rifles and loads being hunted with today have indeed taken modern muzzleloader performance to a whole new level.

The innovative in-line ignition front-loader that definitely crosses over into the realm of center-fire performance with some of its hotter loads is the .50 caliber Savage Model 10ML II. At last, here is a front-loaded

Modern smokeless powders like IMR-4227, Accurate Arms XMP5744 and VihtaVuori N110 can be used in Savage's revolutionary Model 10ML II rifle.

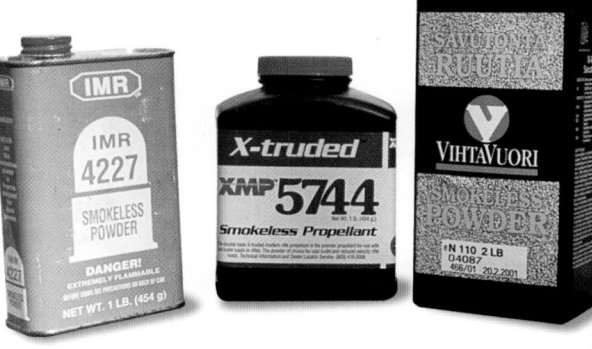

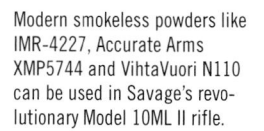

TYPICAL SMOKELESS LOADS FOR SAVAGE MODEL 10ML II > 24-INCH .50 CALIBER BARREL

BULLET	POWDER/CHARGE	MUZZLE VELOCITY	MUZZLE ENERGY
250 gr. Hornady .452" SST/Hornady Sabot	43 gr. IMR-SR4759	2,335 f.p.s.	3,025 f.p.e.
300 gr. Hornady .452" SST/Hornady Sabot	43 gr. IMR-SR4759	2,227 f.p.s.	3,300 f.p.e.
250 gr. Hornady .452" XTP/MMP "HP" Sabot	46 gr. IMR-4227	2,147 f.p.s.	2,550 f.p.e.
300 gr. Hornady .452" XTP/MMP "HP" Sabot	46 gr. IMR-4227	2,080 f.p.s.	2,880 f.p.e.
250 gr. Parker .451" Hydra-Con/MMP "HP" Sabot	45 gr. Accurate Arms XMP5744	2,227 f.p.s.	2,750 f.p.e.
275 gr. Parker .451" Hydra-Con/MMP "HP" Sabot	45 gr. Accurate Arms XMP5744	2,196 f.p.s.	2,942 f.p.e.
250 gr. Hornady .452" SST/Hornady Sabot	44.5 gr. VihtaVuori N110	2,368 f.p.s.	3,100 f.p.e.
300 gr. Hornady .452" SST/Hornady Sabot	44.5 gr. VihtaVuori N110	2,244 f.p.s.	3,360 f.p.e.

.50 RIFLE

The author dumped this big Midwestern whitetail buck in his tracks at 150 yards with a 45-grain charge of VihtaVuori N110 and a saboted 250-grain Hornady .452 XTP. The load gives 2,392 f.p.s. at the muzzle and generates 3,175 foot-pounds of energy.

big game rifle that has been built with the design integrity and strength to safely consume effective charges of modern nitrocellulose-based powders. In fact, some of the same powders used to load favorite center-fire big game cartridges like the old .30/30 Winchester, .35 Remington and .444 Marlin are proving capable of amazing accuracy and knockdown power out of the Savage muzzleloader—and without all of the mess generally associated with shooting muzzle-loaded rifles.

The Savage Model 10ML II system has been found to turn in its best performance with medium burn-rate powders that are just a little on the fast side of that scale. Some of the best-producing powders include IMR-4227, IMR-SR4759, Accurate Arms XMP (XMR) 5744, and VihtaVuori N110. For the most part, a 44- to 45-grain charge of these powders will produce velocities of around 2,100 to nearly 2,400 f.p.s. with a saboted 250-grain bullet. And shooters who are well satisfied with the lower velocities of Pyrodex and black powder loads, can turn to slightly slower burning powders such as Alliant Reloder 7 and VihtaVuori N120. With 45 to 47 grains of these powders, the Model 10ML II will get a 250-grain saboted bullet out of the muzzle at around 1,950 f.p.s. And it does so with hardly any recoil and no worry of corrosive fouling.

The advantages of shooting nitrocellulose-based powders out of this muzzleloader also include a much lower cost per shot. Out of a pound can of FFg black powder, a shooter can get 70 charges weighing 100 grains. When shooting Pyrodex RS/Select, you can add another 23 or 24 shots since the powder is 30 percent bulkier. Those powders retail for around $20 per pound. Now, a pound can of IMR-4227 sells for about the same. And out of that pound can, a shooter can get 155 shots when loading with 45 grains. Shooting the smokeless charges costs about half of what it costs to shoot black powder, and is 40 percent cheaper than shooting loose-grain Pyrodex.

The somewhat downside of shooting smokeless loads out of the Model 10ML II is that these loads must be more precise than with other "softer pushing" powders. If a charge varies as much as a half-grain, point of impact can change several inches. However, the shooter who takes time to precisely weigh charges on a scale will find this rifle to produce unbelievable accuracy at 100 to 200 yards. Still, charges can be easily measured with the simple Lee Precision plastic measure dippers and produce solid 1½-inch, 100-yard groups. And with loads that top 2,300 f.p.s., trajectory becomes as flat as a muzzleloader is likely to ever produce. When shooting a very aerodynamic bullet, like the 250-grain Hornady SST, a 10ML II can be sighted 2 inches high at 100 yards, and the shot will only be 3 inches below point of aim at 200 yards. This would allow a dead-on hold from up close all the way out to 200 yards.

NOTE: The Savage Model 10ML II is currently the only production muzzleloader designed and built to shoot smokeless powders. The higher pressures created by these powders could destroy any other muzzleloader.

Compressed Pyrodex or Triple Seven Pellets make loading easier and quicker, eliminating the need to precisely measure a charge of loose-grain powder.

Putting It All Together

Finding the right powder and bullet combination for your rifle are definitely two major steps to getting the performance you're looking for. Often it takes a great deal of experimenting with different powders and bullets before a shooter finds the optimum load for a particular rifle. Other times, the first combination shoots so good, some never experiment any further.

Each of us has a different level of acceptance. If you feel confident that you can take every game animal you shoot at with a rifle and load that can only shoot inside of 3 inches at 100 yards, and you're happy with that, I'm sure you'll enjoy many successful seasons. Just know your limitations, and the limitations of the muzzleloader and load you hunt with. Shoot it often enough to know exactly how it prints on paper, and at what point you feel uncertain about hitting a big game well enough to cleanly bring it down. If you've never shot your rifle at 200 yards, ask yourself, "Should I shoot at a nice buck at 200 yards?" The answer lies within you.

the
"NIFTY" FIFTY

To determine just which muzzle-loaded bore size is the most popular to-day, all you have to do is walk into any large gun shop that offers a great selection of muzzleloader accessories, and take a look at the variety of projectiles now offered. The selection available for the .50 caliber rifles will easily be three or four times greater than the number of choices offered for the .45 and .54 caliber rifles combined. Or, you can thumb through the catalog section of a big gun annual, such as *Shooter's Bible,* and you'll see that far more high performance muzzleloading big game rifles are offered in .50 caliber than any other caliber. In fact, there are quite a few very popular models that are now offered in .50 caliber only.

American muzzleloading hunters have had a love affair with the half-inch bore for about 30 years, primarily starting with the .50 caliber Thompson/Center Arms "Hawken" rifle during the early 1970s. There were a few earlier reproductions offered in that caliber, but the guns just did not appeal to the shooting public as well as the attractive brass-mounted and walnut stocked T/C Hawken. What helped win this 28-inch barreled half-stock a reputation as a hunter's rifle was its fast handling short length (for a muzzle-loader anyway) and the fact that its designer, Warren Center, also designed right along with the rifle a hard-hitting conical bullet known as the "Maxi-Ball." The combination of the T/C Hawken and 370-grain bore-sized .50 caliber bullet quickly won a reputation for being lethal on big game. And by the late 1970s, more muzzleloading hunters toted this rifle and heavy projectile into the deer woods than any other design or make.

Like many shooters who had been bitten by the muzzleloading bug during the early 1960s, I, too, abandoned my old long-barreled .45 caliber Kentucky for one of the shorter and much harder-hitting .50 caliber half-stock rifles. My original load for the gun was 100 grains of FFg black powder, which got the big chunk of soft lead out of the muzzle at around 1,420

FAR LEFT: Renowned muzzle-loading big game hunter Jim Shockey used a .50 caliber Knight in-line rifle to harvest every species of North American big game. He took this muzzle-loading record book pronghorn buck with an early prototype of the Knight D.I.S.C. Rifle.

BELOW: Gerry Blair used a .50 caliber Knight MK-85 loaded with a saboted 260-grain Speer to take the then World Record muzzleloader elk in 1990.

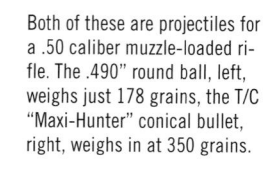

Both of these are projectiles for a .50 caliber muzzle-loaded rifle. The .490" round ball, left, weighs just 178 grains, the T/C "Maxi-Hunter" conical bullet, right, weighs in at 350 grains.

f.p.s., with just over 1,650 ft. lbs. of energy. The load would retain right at 1,200 foot-pounds of energy out at 100 yards, three times the amount of energy possible with my old .45 longrifle, and more than twice as much energy as the .50 caliber Hawken itself loaded with a patched 178-grain .490" round ball. It was this rifle and bullet that signaled the end of round ball popularity.

Presently, muzzleloading rifles in .50 caliber now account for more than three-fourths of the total number of front-loaded hunting rifles manufactured in and imported to the United States. And of those guns, nearly 80 percent of them are now of the modern in-line ignition design. If you are asking yourself why, the answer is simple. Through the past three decades, this bore size has proven itself to be the most versatile, and as the variety of projectiles for the .50 caliber bore is further expanded and improved, this caliber will just keep on growing in popularity.

The true versatility of the .50 caliber came to light with the introduction of the plastic sabot system. Before that, shooters were pretty well limited to shooting either a patched round ball of .490" or .495" diameter, weighing 178 to 180 grains, or one of several heavy lead bore-sized concial bullets ranging from about 350 to 425 grains. With the Muzzleload Magnum Products sabot system, which first came to the market in 1984, the modern-day hunter found available a wide range of .44 and .45 caliber pistol or handgun cartridge projectiles that could be loaded into and shot out of a .50 caliber front-loading rifle. Even during the early years of muzzleloader sabot use, the performance-minded hunter could still find good shooting bullets of 180 to 300 grains readily available from companies like Sierra, Speer, Nosler, Hornady and a few other bullet makers.

Strangely, when the sabot system was first introduced there were very, very few bores in commercial production that were actually well suited for the system. The popular Thompson/Center Arms "Hawken" still featured a turn-in-48 inches

Outdoor writer Jim Shockey outfits hunts for big black bears on Vancouver Island, British Columbia, and took this 500-pound plus brute with one shot with a saboted 300-grain bullet from his Knight MK-85 rifle.

rate of rifling twist. And even the very first of the modernistic Knight MK-85 in-line rifles were built with the same rate of rifling twist, which was more suited to shooting either the patched round ball or conical bullet like the T/C "Maxi-Ball."

In 1985, I met Tony Knight for the first time, when he invited me to his northern Missouri farm to do some shooting with his new in-line design. I took a custom half-stock side-hammer I had built around a much faster custom cut turn-in-24 inches rate of rifling twist .50 caliber barrel. By the time I headed back home after several days of shooting the first MK-85 rifles with conical bullets like the new 385-grain Buffalo Bullet Company hollow-based and hollow-pointed bullet, as well as a variety of bullets through my faster twist barrel, including saboted bullets of 240 and 260 grains, Knight was convinced that it would take a combination of such saboted loads and a fast-twist in-line ignition mounted barrel to set the stage for the future of muzzleloading. By late spring the next year, the MK-85s were sporting a new barrel with a stepped-up turn-in-32 inches rate of twist. And a little more than a year later, Knight went to a still faster turn-in-28 inches twist.

The author with a record book class Wyoming mule deer, dropped with a single shot from his .50 caliber Knight MK-85 at just over 150 yards.

While saboted bullets also proved popular out of fast-twist .45 and .54 caliber rifles, it was the nifty fifty that tended to deliver the performance the muzzleloding big game hunter was seeking. Loaded with 90 or 100 grains of FFFg black powder or Pyrodex RS/Select, an early .50 caliber Knight MK-85 would get bullets of around 250 grains out of the muzzle at around 1,600 f.p.s., generating around 1,450 f.p.e. At 100 yards, a really good load would consistently shoot inside of 2½ inches and hit with around 1,100 f.p.e. And the loads shot with little if any recoil, plus the hunter who might be faced with a 150-yard shot only had to contend with around a 6- or 7-inch drop, not the 12 to 14 inches of drop with either the round ball or heavy lead conical bullet. Muzzleloader hunters had never had it so good.

The performance levels of those early saboted bullet loads are a far cry from the velocities, energies, accuracy and trajectory now possible with the more advanced in-line ignition rifles, hotter powders and vastly improved bullet designs now favored by the majority of modern-day muzzleloading hunters. Here is a look at some of the more popular current .50 caliber models and the loads that make them superior to any muzzle-loaded big game rifle ever offered at anytime in the past.

The new leader when it comes to muzzleloading performance is the .50 caliber Savage Model 10ML II rifle. What gives this 24-inch barreled front-loader a performance edge over any other modern in-line muzzleloader is that here is the only rifle of its type designed and built to be loaded and shot with significantly hotter smokeless powders. With 45-grain charges of nitrocellulose-based powders like IMR-4227, Accurate Arms XMP5744 and VihtaVuori N110, this hot new muzzleloader is capable of getting a saboted 250-grain bullet out of the muzzle at velocities approaching 2,400 f.p.s., generating nearly 3,300 f.p.e. And with extremely aerodynamic bullets with a high ballistic coefficient, such as the Hornady SST or Parker Hydra-Con, some of these loads can retain 1,700 to 1,900 foot-pounds of energy all the way out at 200 yards.

A .50 caliber in-line with a fast-twist bore can be loaded with a magnum charge of Pyrodex or Triple Seven behind a heavy saboted bullet or bore-sized conical and deliver the punch needed to bring down game even as large as a buffalo (bison) bull.

When it comes to all other models that must still be loaded with black powder, Pyrodex or Triple Seven powders, the Omega drop action rifle from Thompson/Center Arms is the top performer. The 28-inch barrel of this modern in-line gives it a slight velocity and energy edge over other in-lines with 24- or 26-inch barrels. The longer bore of the Omega simply gives a magnum powder charge more room to be completely consumed, resulting in more push on the rear of the sabot and projectile. And while this rifle shoots very well with a 150-grain charge of Pyrodex Pellets or Triple Seven Pellets, its best velocity will come when loaded with 120 to 140 grains of loose-grain FFFg Triple Seven behind a saboted bullet. In fact, the author has gotten one of the saboted 250-grain T/C Shock Wave polymer-tipped spire-point bullets out of the muzzle of the Omega at just over 2,200 f.p.s. with 140 grains of FFFg Triple Seven. That's 2,700+ f.p.e.!

Most other No. 209 primer ignited .50 caliber in-line rifle models, such as the Knight D.I.S.C. Extreme or the New England Firearms Huntsman, easily get a saboted 250-grain bullet out of the muzzle of a 24- to 26-inch barrel at around 2,000 f.p.s. with a 100-grain charge of FFFg Triple Seven, or 150-grain charge of Pyrodex or Triple Seven Pellets. Thanks to the improvements made to sabots, bullets and even the rifles over the past 20 years, most of these guns are fully capable of printing 1½-inch, 100-yard groups with these hard-hitting loads.

The variety of saboted bullets now available for today's modern .50 caliber in-line rifles is nothing short of mind boggling. Hornady, Thompson/Center Arms, Barnes, Nosler, Speer, Winchester, Buffalo Bullet Company, Precision Rifle Custom Muzzleloader Bullets, Traditions, Knight Rifles, Swift Bullet Company and

quite a few other suppliers now package saboted bullets for the .50 caliber from around 180 grains all the way up to more than 400 grains. And if close-range knockdown power is of more importance to you than pinpoint long-range accuracy, companies like White Rifles and Parker Productions offer big, soft lead conical bullets up to around 600 grains for the .50 caliber bores. Now, if you can get one of these out of the muzzle at 1,400 f.p.s., the load will generate right at 2,600 f.p.e.

There is currently a bullet weight and design available that's ideal for just about any hunting situation or hunter's need. And when time is taken to work up the optimum powder charge for that bullet and .50 caliber rifle, the combination can prove to be a tack driver that slams home with tremendous knockdown power.

Like the vast majority of muzzleloading hunters in this country, noted outdoor television show host David Hale favors a modern in-line .50 caliber for his big game hunting.

is the .54 a true "POWERHOUSE"?

Big half-stocked plains rifles from the 1840s, like the St. Louis-made Hawken rifles, popularized the larger .52- to .54 caliber bores. Westward travelers headed from Missouri for the Pacific coast, and all points in between, were to be faced with bigger and often more dangerous game, like the grizzly bear. They needed a rifle with the stopping power to get the job done. Likewise, a hungry pioneer who had just crawled up on a 2,000-pound bison more than likely felt a little under-gunned when sighting down the long barrel of his favorite, and probably only, long-barreled .44 caliber Kentucky rifle.

Although early development of harder-hitting conical bullets had already begun about the time settlers started the movement west, rifles that shot bullets well were still far and few between. The round ball continued to be the most widely used projectile, and when those eastern hunters first encountered game that could weigh from a half-ton to more than a ton on the hoof, "Ol' Betsy," which had been barely adequate on 200-pound whitetails, more often than not probably failed to cleanly bring down such really big game—if it brought it down at all.

Back then, little, if anything, was really known about internal or external ballistics. Something either worked or it didn't work. In regards to rifle efficiency, if a caliber was adequate or inadequate for the task at hand, the word spread quickly. Rifle makers of the time built and sold muzzleloaders to the needs of those who would be using them. And many a western mountain man and settler likely owed their lives to the fact that they got rid of their "squirrel rifle" in favor of a larger bore plains rifle, which in essence was the high performance muzzleloader of the period.

FAR LEFT: The traditionally styled Thomspon/Center Arms .54 caliber Hawken rifle used to take this whitetail buck generates enough energy for the task with either the patched round ball or bore-sized conical bullet. The latter just maintains that energy level about twice as far as the lead sphere.

BELOW: When hunting really big game like moose or elk with the .54 caliber rifles, even a 220-grain ball propelled by 120 grains of black powder won't maintain enough energy to ensure a clean harvest much past 60 or 70 yards.

The .54 vs. the .45 and .50

Although records kept by Jacob and Samuel Hawken are somewhat sketchy, and questionable, the gunmakers are said to have recommended starting loads for any of their rifles to be a powder charge that was half the weight of the ball. The author has read the accounts of one Hawken rifle owner who did just that, starting his loads with 108 grains of FFFg black powder behind the 216-grain ball for his .53

caliber Hawken built plains rifle. He then worked up from there, all the way to 205 grains of powder! Since an original Hawken rifle in .53 caliber was not available, we'll look at what kind of velocity and knockdown energy is possible with a .54 caliber heavy-barreled (34-inch) half-stock rifle loaded with heavy powder charges and a slightly heavier 220-grain ball. All the loads listed were actually shot out of a .54 custom Hawken rifle with charges of FFFg GOEX black powder.

No .54 caliber shooter would even think about starting with a powder charge less than 100 grains. Using that amount of GOEX FFFg black powder, a 220-grain tightly patched round ball is pushed from the muzzle of the 34-inch barrel at 1,639 f.p.s. That translates into 1,310 f.p.e. Upping the amount of powder to 120 grains of FFFg brings the velocity up to 1,826 f.p.s., with 1,628 f.p.e. Moving on up to 140 grains of FFFg, the velocity moves up accordingly to 1,972 f.p.s., generating 1,898 f.p.e. And going to 160 grains of FFFg gets that 220-grain ball out of the muzzle at 2,072 f.p.s., with an impressive 2,094 f.p.e.

Any .44 to .45 caliber longrifle that started westward with settlers from Penn-

This hunter accepted the challenge of getting close enough with his round ball loaded flintlock .54 caliber to take his bull. Knowing and adhering to the established maximum effective range of this projectile is the key to prevent losing wounded game.

sylvania, Virginia, and the Carolinas would probably not have been stoked with any more than 70 grains of FFFg black powder. With a lengthy 40- to 44-inch barrel, such charges would send a 120- to 130-grain ball moving at about 1,970 f.p.s. However, due to the light weight of the round projectiles, the load would only generate around 1,100 f.p.e. Moving up to a 90-grain charge would up the velocity to around 2,250 f.p.s. and the energy to around 1,475 f.p.e. As impressive as that may seem for such a small bore, in the open country of the West, this load would drop energy at 100 yards to around 400 to 450 foot-pounds of knockdown power.

Original eastern rifles with bores that had been re-bored and re-rifled might have had a bore closer to .50 caliber (.47 and .48 caliber re-cut bores were fairly common). With an 80-grain charge of FFFg behind a patched 170- to 175-grain ball, the load would have given around 1,850 f.p.s. from a 40-inch barrel, and would have been good for around 1,330 f.p.e. Even if a 90-grain charge of FFFg was loaded, the velocity would be around 2,000 f.p.s., with about 1,550 f.p.e.

When it came to saving one's life from a charging grizzly or downing enough buffalo meat to feed a wagon train full of settlers using early round ball loads, the old behemoth .54 caliber rifles were definitely the guns to be carrying. Even so, when compared to the ballistics possible with modern loads in an equally modern .54 caliber big game rifle, or even a .50 for that matter, the guns and loads that settled the West might seem awfully inadequate.

Loaded with a 110-grain charge of Pyrodex "RS/Select" and a saboted 275-grain Barnes all-copper Expander MZ, the author's .54 caliber Knight Magnum Elite dropped this nice Nebraska buck where he stood. The distance of the shot was just 50 yards.

Modern .54 Caliber Rifles and Loads

More recently, .54 caliber rifles enjoyed a heyday during the late 1970s and early 1980s. It was during this period that some of the first muzzleloader only elk seasons were established, and it didn't take modern-day hunters long to realize that their .50 caliber rifles often lacked the oomph needed to bring down an animal that could weigh 700 to 900 pounds. This was especially true if the shooter was hunting with a patched round ball.

A large number of so-called Hawken reproductions captured a lion's share of the muzzleloading market. About as many of these rifles were sold in .54 as the overall more popular .50 caliber. While most serious muzzleloading hunters never hunted elk, it was nevertheless the dream of most to do so some day. Step one was to own a rifle that could deliver the knockdown power needed.

Many of the reproduction front-loaders built during this period closely followed the lines of original guns, produced to satisfy a growing interest in the historical side of muzzleloading, known as buckskinning. And to satisfy their desires to own a muzzleloader as authentically styled as possible, quite a few of these .54 caliber guns were offered with a slow one turn-in-66 inches (and slower) rate of rifling twist for shooting the patched round ball. But not all...

It was during this period that the Thompson/Center Hawken became the most popular muzzle-loaded hunting rifle in America. And T/C elected to offer the .54 caliber version with the same turn-in-48 inches rifling found in the smaller .45 and .50 caliber versions. Out of these rifles, hunters looking to harvest game as large as elk, moose and bears turned to huge .54 caliber soft lead conical bullets that could weigh 450 grains or more.

Loaded with a 120-grain charge of FFg black powder and one of T/C's own 430-grain "Maxi-Ball" bullets, the 28-inch-barreled Hawken rifle is good for 1,499 f.p.s. at the muzzle. While not a real speedster, the big bullet has a lot of mass, and once that mass is moving, even at that relatively slow velocity, it pro-

The Knight Magnum Elite, of the mid-1990s, was one of the finer .54 caliber in-line rifles ever offered.

Saboted .50 caliber bullets, like the big 325-grain Speer jacketed hollow-point, and the Knight 450-grain lead bullets, shown at left, can turn the .54 into a potent 150-yard big game rifle.

duces a whopping 2,146 f.p.e. at the muzzle. For comparison: The same charge of powder will push a patched 224-grain Speer swaged round ball from the muzzle at 1,825 f.p.s., but due to the lighter weight of the ball, the load generates nearly 500 foot-pounds less energy than the heavy conical bullet.

As shooters stoked the big .54 bores with heavier bullets and powder charges, another aspect of shooting .54 became evident—the painful recoil. Slowly, recoil sensitive shooters began to abandon the .54 and went back to the .50. They discovered that when loaded with similar powder charges, the half-inch bore loaded with a slightly lighter conical bullet could surpass the .54 in velocity, and could nearly match it in the energy department as well.

White Rifles claims that when their 22-inch barrel, .50 caliber Whitetail Model 97 is loaded with a 120-grain charge of Pyrodex "P" (the equivalent of FFFg black powder) and one of their 440-grain PowerPunch conical bullets, the load is good for 1,498 f.p.s. That means, at the muzzle, this .50 caliber is capable of generating 2,143 f.p.e. If a shooter found the recoil from that much powder still too objectionable, the charge could be reduced to 110 grains of Pyrodex "P," and it would still get the 440-grain bullet out of the muzzle at around 1,450 f.p.s., which means the bullet still generates a little more than 2,000 f.p.e. At 200 yards, the load would still clobber a bull elk with nearly 1,000 foot-pounds of knockdown power.

When modern in-line rifles started to replace side-hammer traditional rifles as the hunting rifles of choice during the early 1990s, the .54 caliber bores still accounted for close to 30 percent of the guns being built and sold in this country. However, with the more popular saboted bullets, shooters were fast to realize that the .54 offered no real advantage. Most of the sabot loads available for both the .50 and .54 were offered with the same .429 and .451 bullets. The only thing different was the sabot required to shoot either diameter in the .50 or .54 calibers.

If anything, modern-day shooters found the .54 something of a handicap when loaded with saboted bullets. It stands to reason that to shoot a .452 Hornady 300-grain XTP out of a .54 bore will require a sabot with considerably thicker sleeves or petals than the sabot required to shoot the same bullet from a .50 caliber bore. Time and time again, shooters have proven that a heavier sabot will tend to stick with the bullet longer than a thinner sabot. And many of those shooters gave up on trying to get optimum accuracy with .54 caliber saboted bullets and went back to a .50 caliber. Basically, they found that a .50 caliber in-line loaded with a saboted bullet was capable of doing anything that a .54 caliber rifle and saboted bullet could do, and that, generally, the .50 caliber did it far more accurately.

This isn't to say that you can't get a fast-twist .54 caliber bore to shoot accurately with a saboted bullet. The key lies in shooting a bullet that's as close to bore size as possible. In short, that means forget about all of the .429" diameter bullets and most of the .451" and .452" bullets. The .54 rifles will perform much better when stuffed with a saboted .50 caliber projectile.

One of the best shooting saboted bullets for guns with a turn-in-24 to 28 inches has been the big 325-grain jacketed hollow-point bullet Speer offers for the .50 AE handguns. I once owned a .54 caliber Knight MK-85 with a rare 26-inch barrel that would consistently punch 1½-inch groups at 100 yards when loaded with a

Toby Bridges relied on one of the Knight Magnum Elite .54 caliber in-line rifles and saboted 325-grain Speer jacketed hollow-point to down this Auodad ram at about 140 yards.

110-grain charge of Pyrodex "RS/Select" behind a Speer .50 caliber bullet with a purple Muzzleload Magnum Products .50x.54 sabot. The load was good for 1,590 f.p.s. and 1,823 f.p.e. It was a lethal load for whitetails and elk.

Another great shooting saboted bullet for .54 caliber rifles is the all-copper Barnes Expander MZ. Barnes offers a .500 bullet in two weights (275 and 325 grains) for loading with a sabot. With a 110-grain charge of Pyrodex "RS/Select," the 275-grain bullet can be pushed from the muzzle of a 24-inch barrel at around 1,625 f.p.s., producing around 1,610 f.p.e. Several years ago I hunted with *American Hunter* editor John Zent who used the 325-grain Expander MZ in his Knight .54 caliber in-line to drop a nice 6x6 bull elk at 200 yards.

The .54 is still a great caliber for hunting big game. Today's shooter, however, will find many more bullet choices for the overwhelmingly popular .50 caliber rifles. Only a few in-line rifles are still offered in .54 caliber, and how long they will be, remains to be seen. At this writing, the sales of .54 in-line rifles accounted for less than 10 percent of all high performance muzzleloading big game rifle sales.

ABOVE: At one time, the .54 caliber models accounted for nearly 30 percent of all rifles produced by Knight Rifles. Today, that percentage has dropped to less than 10 percent.

RIGHT: Two custom muzzle-loading big game rifles built by the author are an authentically styled .54 caliber percussion "Hawken" (left) and a semi-modern .50 caliber half-stock hunting rifle (right). The latter was built to shoot modern conical bullets, and will generate considerably more knockdown power than the round ball loads that must be fired from the larger .54 caliber bore.

IS THERE A MARKET FOR A .52 CALIBER?

The past couple of years, Knight Rifles of Centerville, Iowa, has worked hard to try and establish a niche for a modern in-line muzzleloading rifle of .52 caliber. At one time, the .54 caliber accounted for nearly 30 percent of their in-line rifle-making business. However, in the past decade or so, the percentage of .54 rifles produced at their southern Iowa facility has dropped to only just a little over 5 percent. The .50 caliber bore has taken over. In fact, rifles with a true half-inch bore size now account for more than 80 percent of all muzzleloading rifles produced.

When the topic of Knight's new .52 comes up among a group of knowledgeable in-line rifle users, the question most asked is "Why?" The .54 caliber died in popularity for two reasons:

1. The .50 caliber could basically do anything and everything the slightly larger bore could do ballistically, and usually proved more accurate.
2. The .54 was not versatile enough, with fewer good choices of bullets.

Many feel the new .52 is destined to the same demise. Knight contracted with Muzzleload Magnum Products to produce two new sabots specifically for the new bore size. One is a .458x.52 sabot for shooting any of the jacketed .458" bullets currently available. The other sabot, of .475x.52 configuration, has been designed for loading bullets of .475" diameter.

Now, not many bullet makers are offering a large-scale selection of .475" diameter bullets, and quite a few of the .458" bullets currently available have been engineered and constructed for shooting out of big center-fire cartridges like the .458 Winchester Magnum "elephant rifles" and are far too tough to perform at muzzleloader velocities. Even with the massive 150-grain charges of Triple Seven FFFg that Knight promotes, getting a 350- to 400-grain saboted bullet out of the muzzle at velocities much faster than 1,900 f.p.s. will be darn hard.

At one time, the .54 caliber accounted for nearly 30 percent of Knight's in-line sales, but the caliber died. Now the company is trying to make a niche for the .52 caliber.

Knight has contracted with Barnes to produce a 350-grain all-copper addition to their "Red Hot" line of bullets for the new .52 caliber. If a 150-grain charge of Triple Seven FFFg gets the big bullet out of the muzzle at 1,900 f.p.s., it will develop 2,800 f.p.e. That would be one great elk or moose load. However, if a shooter could burn a 150-grain charge of FFFg Triple Seven in his .50 caliber, it would get a 300-grain bullet out of the muzzle at around 2,100 f.p.s., and develop nearly 2,950 f.p.e.

Only time will tell whether Knight can make a go of their .52 caliber. From where I sit, the .50 still seems to be *"King of the Hill."*

what's so super about the "SUPER .45s!"

FAR RIGHT: Today's new breed of Super .45 in-line rifles are ideal for younger shooters who may find the recoil of a larger bore front-loader objectionable. This young hunter used one of the Traditions Lightning LD .45 rifles to take his buck.

In recent years, the .45 caliber bore has enjoyed renewed popularity, thanks to the introduction of much better bullet and sabot designs, plus the development of hotter powders that give the bore size some added zip. At this point, it wouldn't be exactly accurate to say that muzzle-loaded rifles in .45 caliber have gotten a new lease on life, but rather that the muzzleloading hunter willing to refine a load for a rifle of this caliber will find it a very adequate muzzle-loading deer rifle.

Knight, Thompson/Center Arms, Traditions, Connecticut Valley Arms, and a few others, have been beating the .45 drum loudly, claiming that it is a better long-range muzzle-loaded big game rifle than the .50 caliber rifles. This writer doesn't exactly agree with those feelings, but will concede that with a hefty enough powder charge and one of the more advanced saboted bullets, the .45 can indeed live up to the expectations of the performance-minded muzzleloading whitetail or mule deer hunter. And with a bore-sized conical bullet of around 300 grains or more, the .45 can even deliver all the punch needed for downing still larger game, like elk.

One of the finest examples of a Super .45 is the Thompson/Center Arms break-open Encore 209x45 Super Magnum. Part of what makes this lightweight front-loader so neat is that the shooter can purchase accessory barrels in a wide range of center-fire rifle calibers, a shotgun barrel and even a .50 caliber muzzle-loading barrel that will go right on to the Encore pistol and rifle receiver or frame with a minimum of work. However, because of the interchangeability with available modern cartridge barrels, the Encore muzzleloaders require the same paperwork as when buying a modern cartridge-firing firearm.

Thompson/Center claims that when loaded with a 150-grain Pyrodex Pellet powder charge and a saboted 155-grain .40 caliber Hornady XTP jacketed hollow-point bullet, this 26-inch barreled .45 front-loader is good for just over 2,600 f.p.s. at the muzzle. That translates into 2,326 foot-pounds of energy. Now, that's getting close to the muzzle ballistics of the popular .308 Winchester rifles.

So, will this .45 speedster and load perform right along with the .308 once the bullet gets a ways from the muzzle? Well, not exactly. You see, most 150- to 160-grain .30 caliber spire-point bullets for the .308 have a ballistic coefficient of around .350. Most factory loaded ammo gets the bullet out of the muzzle of a 22- to 24-inch barrel at around 2,800 f.p.s., with 2,600 f.p.e. At 100 yards, the bullet is

still flying at around 2,500 f.p.s., retaining 2,100 f.p.e. And out at 200 yards, a 150-grain .30 caliber spire-point maintains a velocity of around 2,300 f.p.s. and hits with close to 1,750 foot-pounds of authority.

The 155-grain .40 caliber Hornady XTP has a ballistic coefficient of just .135, or thereabouts. Given a 2,600 f.p.s. muzzle velocity, the hollow-point will have slowed to around 1,975 f.p.s. at 100 yards, and hit with 1,340 f.p.e. And all the way out at 200 yards, the blunt-nosed and hollow-pointed 155-grain XTP will slow to around 1,450 f.p.s. and hit a whitetail with just 720 foot-pounds of remaining energy. That is hardly a high performance load.

Knight has contracted Barnes Bullets to produce a .40 caliber 195-grain all-copper hollow-pointed spire-point to add to their line-up of Red Hot bullets for the .45 caliber. With a 150-grain charge of Pyrodex Pellets, this bullet can be pushed from the bore of a 26-inch barrel at just over 2,400 f.p.s. At the muzzle, the load is good for 2,492 f.p.e. Thanks to the much higher .230 b.c. of this bullet, at 100 yards it would maintain a velocity of 2,050 f.p.s. and hit with more than 1,800 foot-pounds of knockdown power. And when this load gets to 200 yards, the 195-grain Knight-Barnes bullet would be moving along at just over 1,700 f.p.s. and would maintain right at 1,250 foot-pounds of punch. Or, more than enough to cleanly down even the biggest whitetail or mule deer buck.

It takes more than the ballistics at the muzzle to harvest big game cleanly. While the 155-grain XTP might leave the muzzle of the Encore 209x45 Super Magnum at warp speed, the light weight and poor aerodynamics of the bullet dictate that it will shed much needed velocity and energy quickly downrange—where the performance is really needed. The hunter looking for top performance with a saboted bullet from any of today's so-called "Super" or "Magnum" .45 caliber rifles needs to concentrate on only those bullets with improved aerodynamics and a high ballistic coefficient.

Another great bullet for the .45 is the 200-grain .40 caliber Hornady SST. This modern polymer-tipped jacketed spire-point has a b.c. of around .225. And with a 150-grain charge of Pyrodex or Triple Seven Pellets, this bullet can also be pushed from the muzzle of a 26-inch barrel right at 2,400 f.p.s., generating 2,550 f.p.e. Downrange at 200 yards this load would deliver the 200-grain spire-point with close to 1,300 f.p.e. of energy. The center-fire rifle projectile design of the SST incor-

A short, and handy, .45 caliber like this Markesberry "outer line" rifle is ideal for the hunter who likes to still hunt through his favorite hunting spot.

Loaded with some of today's extremely aerodynamic spire-point bullets with a high ballistic coefficient, some of the new "Magnum" .45 front-loaders are capable of producing extremely flat trajectory out to about 200 yards.

Many of the newer .45 caliber in-lines have won a reputation for their pinpoint accuracy. While not brush busters, the light 150- to 200-grain saboted bullets these rifles are loaded with can be threaded through small openings to hit right where they need to go.

porates a jacket that tapers in thickness from the base to the tip. When this bullet hits, the tough polymer tip is pushed rearward into a shallow internal hollow cavity, causing the thinner forward portion of the jacket to peel out and backward to encourage exceptional expansion. Hornady also incorporates their "Inter-Lock Ring" in this bullet to prevent it from overexpanding and shedding the copper jacket when hitting hair, hide, muscle and bone at higher velocities.

Out of a custom-built .45 caliber Henry Ball "smokeless muzzleloader," this author has used a 43-grain charge of VihtaVuori N110 to get the 200-grain Hornady SST out of the muzzle at a whopping 2,647 f.p.s. Now, that load produces 3,100 foot-pounds of knockdown power at the muzzle, and thanks to the .225 b.c. of this bullet it will hit a big game animal at 200 yards with more than 1,600 f.p.e. Currently, Savage Arms is the only company producing a production smokeless powder muzzleloader, the Model 10ML II. However, this rifle is only available in .50 caliber. If Savage has been waiting until a bullet was developed that would tap the performance of .45 smokeless loads, the 200-grain Hornady SST is that bullet. As this was being written, the bullet maker also planned to introduce a 180-grain .40 caliber SST bullet for the .45 caliber rifles.

Precision Rifle Custom Muzzleloader Bullets, of Manitoba, Canada, currently offers saboted bullets with some of the highest ballistic coefficients currently available. For the .45 caliber bores, the company produces a saboted .357" diameter 175-grain polymer-tipped Dead Center spire-point with a b.c. of .342. Precision Rifle claims that a 100-grain charge of FFFg Triple Seven will get this bullet out of the muzzle at 2,142 f.p.s. That works out to 1,783 f.p.e. Thanks to the unbelievably high b.c. of the 175-grain bullet, the load would still be cranking at around 1,920 f.p.s. at 100 yards, and hit with around 1,475 f.p.e. And at 200 yards, the company says the load is still good for 1,706 f.p.s., with more than 1,100 f.p.e. Not bad for a 175-grain bullet.

Del Ramsey, owner of Muzzleload Magnum Products, produces the sabots for Precision Rifle (and many others) and used this bullet to take the best muzzleloader buck of his life a couple of seasons back. He shot the deer at about 80 yards, and the 175-grain Dead Center practically dropped the buck on the spot. Precision Rifle also offers polymer-tipped 200-grain (.300 b.c.) and 300-grain (.336 b.c.) .40 caliber bullets for loading with a sabot in a .45 caliber rifle. However, if you prefer a "jacketed" bullet, these are not the bullets for you. These are very precisely swaged soft lead bullets.

The .45 caliber loaded with a saboted bullet of 180- to 200 grains is more than a match for most whitetail hunting situations, provided it's stoked with enough powder to generate needed velocity and energy levels.

Where legal, the 300-grain Precision Rifle bullet could turn the .45 caliber bore into a potent larger game rifle. With a 110-grain charge of FFFg Triple Seven, the big bullet is pushed from a 24-inch barrel at 1,880 f.p.s. and is good for 2,352 f.p.e. It would take a 150-grain Pyrodex Pellet load to produce basically the same ballistics with a saboted 300-grain bullet out of a .50 caliber bore.

About 15 years ago, I accompanied a hunting partner as he went for Alaskan moose with his .45 caliber Knight MK-85. He was shooting a 110-grain charge of FFg black powder behind one of the 430-grain White bore-sized lead

ABOVE: Many critics of the .45 maintain that the caliber lost favor among hunters 40 years ago for a reason, the caliber was inadequate for big game. Some feel that it is, at best, a suitable caliber for varmints, like this coyote.

LEFT: The very first whitetail the author ever shot with a modern in-line rifle was taken with this early .45 caliber Knight MK-85. The deer was shot at about 80 yards with a saboted 180-grain bullet, and went less than 50 yards after being hit.

conical bullets. The load was good for only around 1,475 f.p.s. at the muzzle. But thanks to the heavy weight of the bullet, the load developed nearly 1,900 f.p.e. And when he managed to slip within 60 yards of a huge 62-inch bull moose and placed that soft lead bullet right behind the shoulder, the nearly 1,400 pounds of moose traveled less than 100 yards before going down.

If a .45 caliber muzzleloader is your rifle of choice, or if there is a .45 caliber in your future, just remember that it is not speed that kills, it's the amount of energy produced and retained that does the job. Choose your bullet wisely and know the outermost limitations of the load you shoot. Precise bullet placement becomes especially critical when shooting light bullets of around 150 grains.

CHAPTER 11

LOADING
for success

By now, I'm sure you are fully aware that muzzleloading has gone hi-tech. Today's muzzleloading rifles, powders and projectiles are easily more advanced than anything that has ever been offered in the past. Likewise, the performance produced by these front-loaded hunting rifles borders on unbelievable, not only matching but surpassing the range, accuracy and knockdown power of many center-fire cartridge rifles. Tapping this performance not only requires finding the optimum powder, charge and bullet for a given rifle, but very often learning how to load these components for top velocity and accuracy.

FAR LEFT: Believe it or not, traditional muzzleloader packing hunters once headed for the deer woods with a "possibles bag" nearly stuffed this full.

Consistency always has its rewards. And with a modern high performance muzzleloading big game rifle it is usually better accuracy…better bullet speed …and more knockdown power.

The quality of today's muzzleloading components has now caught up with the quality of the components used to hand-load precision center-fire rifle ammo. It hasn't been that long ago when no one seemed to care if a batch of soft lead round balls were .002" to .003" off in diameter, whether a conical bullet was "truly" round, or if the fire from percussion caps was exactly the same from lot to lot. After all, these components were only for loading a muzzleloading rifle. For most, close was good enough 20 or so years ago. Well, not anymore! To get the degree of accuracy most shooters seek today requires very consistent loading components, and precise loading techniques.

Shortly before this book was written, one of the muzzleloading rifle manufacturers contracted me to do some extensive shooting with their rifle loaded with the then new Triple Seven Pellets. They wanted to know the kind of velocities I could obtain with a variety of bullets, how the pellets compared with Pyrodex Pellets, and the accuracy possible. I acquired a good supply of the pellets, and headed for the range. Shooting 100- (2 pellets) and 150-grain (3 pellets) equivalent loads, I was less than impressed with my initial accuracy and velocity spread. With the two-pellet load, I could usually keep hits inside of 1¾ inches at 100 yards, but when I went to the "magnum" three-pellet load, groups tended to open up to 2¼ to 2½ inches.

Now, this isn't all that bad, but I knew the rifle was capable of 1-inch groups. I just couldn't get the tight clusters with the out-of-the-box pellets.

Then I weighed the pellets to see just how much they actually weighed. The so-called 50-grain pellets actually weighed right at 30 grains. And when I ran the entire box of 100 pellets across my electronic scale, I discovered that there was a 2.3 grain variation high to low with the pellets in that box. Meaning that with a 100-grain two-pellet load, my charge could be as much as 4.6 grains off, and as much as 6.9 grains off with the 150-grain three-pellet load. And once I sorted the pellets into lots that were within two-tenths of a grain, I went back to the range and managed to shoot some very impressive 1-inch, 100-yard groups.

Now, some of you are probably saying to yourselves, "I don't want to get into weighing all of my components…that's why I went to pelletized powder charges in the first place!"

If you are perfectly happy with three-shot groups at 100 yards that average 2 to 2½ inches across center to center, then you probably shouldn't have to ever weigh a thing. Just drop in two or three Pyrodex or Triple Seven Pellets, pull a Knight Red Hot bullet from the package and seat the projectile over the powder charge, cap or prime the ignition system and take the shot. As long as you are following the simple basics of muzzleloading, like snapping a cap or primer before loading the first shot, wiping the bore between shots, and using proper seating pressure on the projectile, you should expect to keep the majority of your hits reasonably close to your point of aim. That is, given the powder charge and the bullet diameter/sabot are compatible with your rifle.

However, if you strive for shooting groups that are closer—much closer—to an inch across, you are going to be faced with weighing some of your components very closely. Just as powder pellets can vary in weight, so can a given volume of powder from shot to shot. Not all powder granules are the same size, and when a canister of black powder, Pyrodex or Triple Seven is jostled around, the finer granules will definitely filter to the bottom. The results are powder charges from the bottom of the can that can be significantly hotter than charges measured from the top. More of the finer powder can be gotten into a volumetric powder measure, resulting in a heavier load. However, if charges are actually measured by weight, the amount of difference is reduced significantly. Keep in mind that Pyrodex or Triple Seven charges measured by weight should be reduced 25 to 30 percent. These powders are bulkier than black powder, and are usually measured on a volume-to-volume basis with denser black powder, not by actual weight. A 100-grain volume charge of Triple Seven actually only weighs around 70 grains by weight.

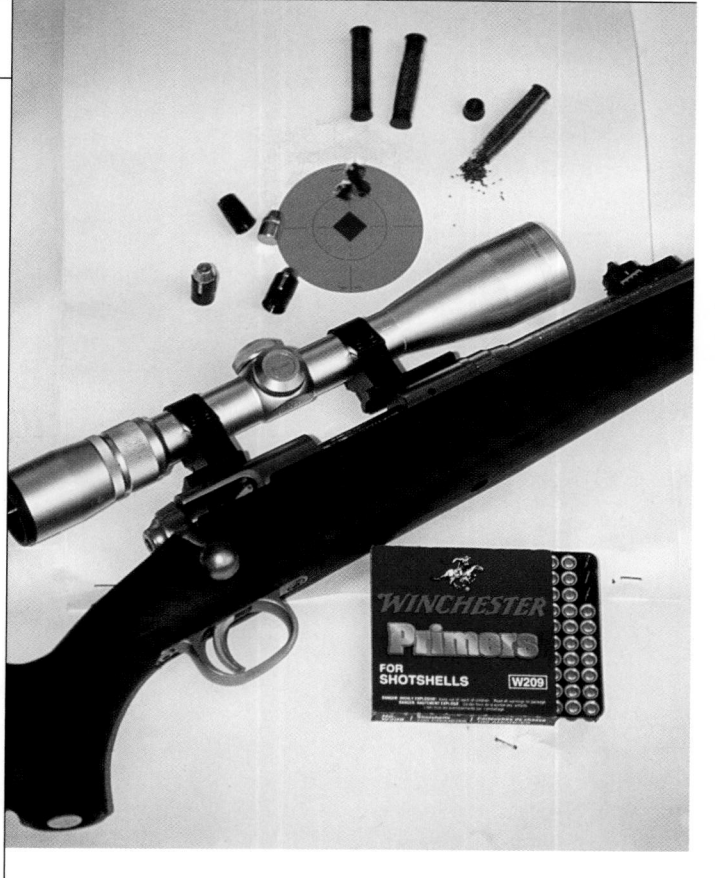

Today's muzzleloading hunter likes things a lot simpler. The loads for this Savage Model 10ML II smokeless muzzleloader are carried in small plastic vials (top right), taking up little room in a jacket pocket.

Many shooters now also run their bullets across the scales as well, separating them into lots that are within ⅓ to ½ grain of each other. Now, if a box of 100 Hornady 250-grain .452" XTP jacketed hollow-point bullets have a maximum spread of only about 1 grain from high to low, this doesn't mean that they are going to print all over the target when loaded with a sabot just as they come out of the box. Instead, all it means to those shooters looking to obtain those lovely one-hole, 100-yard groups is that by weighing and separating the bullets so closely, they have eliminated one of the variables that can result in a bullet impacting an inch or so to one side of the others. However, if a bullet is found to be 2 to 3 grains off from the given weight, chances are there is something wrong with it internally. Discard it and you won't be wasting an expensive powder charge, sabot and primer to only be disappointed.

High Velocity Loads

It hasn't been that many years ago when I was elated to top 1,700 f.p.s. with a saboted 260-grain .451" Speer jacketed hollow-point with a 100-grain charge of Pyrodex "P" out of my first Knight stainless steel .50 caliber MK-85. For several years, I had been shooting just 90 grains of Pyrodex "RS" behind the bullet, for about 1,590 f.p.s. And I had taken a truckload of deer with the rifle and load at ranges out to about 150 yards. With the hotter load of Pyrodex "P," I felt, at the time, that the rifle was then an honest 200-yard deer rifle—provided I could determine the range and the proper holdover.

Today's 150-grain black powder equivalent charges of Pyrodex and Triple Seven Pellets are now pushing saboted bullets of around 240 grains, and lighter, out of the muzzle of a .50 caliber rifle at velocities well over 2,000 f.p.s.! It has not been that many years ago when most muzzleloading rifle makers had established loads of around 100 grains as the maximum load for their rifles. Now, practically everyone in the in-line rifle-making business is touting the use of 150-grain black powder equivalent charges. On many of these rifles, the exact same barrels, ignition system and receiver are still being used. The only thing that has changed has been the performance claims in the advertising and promotional materials!

The magnum charges now widely used are creating significantly greater internal pressures. A 100-grain charge of Pyrodex "RS" behind a saboted 250-grain bullet generates around 13,000 p.s.i. inside the barrel.

One of the hotter 150-grain pellet charges of Triple Seven pushes that pressure level up to 25,000+ p.s.i. Not only are such loads taxing the construction of some rifles, they are also asking an awful lot of the tiny plastic cup that holds the bullet and seals off all of that pressure.

Sabot failure was a big problem during the late 1990s when more and more shooters began to pop in three of the Pyrodex Pellets behind their favorite saboted hunting bullet. This was especially true when trying to sight in a rifle during hot summer months. When temperatures get into the upper 80s and 90s, it takes only a few shots to heat up a big-bore muzzleloader barrel. And when it is that hot, that barrel doesn't cool down too quickly, even if the rifle is placed in the shade. When I worked for Knight Rifles during the mid-1990s, we referred to July and August as "The Silly Season." Getting accuracy from the usually extremely accurate Knight in-line rifles at this time of the year became increasingly more difficult.

TOP: Speed-load tubes, such as these from Traditions, carry a charge of powder and the bullet in separate compartments. With three loaders in one pocket and a capper in another, a hunter is ready for a morning or afternoon on a favorite stand.

BOTTOM: Speed loaders not only offer the convenience of carrying premeasured charges, they also allow the hunter to better ensure the consistency of those loads. Note the short starter feature on this loader.

A plastic sabot has a tough job to perform. The material must be soft enough for the side of the sabot to expand into the rifling when the round is rammed down the bore, but the material must also be resilient enough to hold up to the pressures and heat created by the burning powder charge. Few of the sabots available through the 1990s could fill that bill. Fortunately, the higher performance demands of muzzle-loaded rifles has forced sabot makers to step up to the plate and come up with tougher, yet loadable plastic sabots that can withstand the pressure.

Even with the improved design and polymer materials, heat is still the number one enemy of the plastic sabot. When loaded into a hot barrel and left for just a minute or two, the plastic softens and when the powder charge ignites, a softer sabot will not perform the same as a stiffer sabot. In a really hot barrel, when the plastic is extremely soft, the cupped skirt at the rear of a sabot may not be able to contain the pressure, and the sabot will fail allowing the gasses to escape around the bullet. When this happens, accuracy is totally lost.

Those shooters who use the smokeless powder loads in the Savage .50 caliber Model 10ML II are particularly susceptible to this problem. That's because these loads develop still higher pressure levels that can top 40,000 p.s.i. with some of the hotter powders and charges. These shooters are the "wildcatters" of muzleloading and are discovering ways to harness the power of smokeless powder loads.

A simple solution has been to use a sub-base of some sort to absorb some of the beating delivered by the hotter loads. A variety of approaches have been used, including placing a heavy card disc over the powder charge and following up with one or two wool cushion wads, then the sabot and bullet. Another approach has been to clip the sleeves or petals off of a high-pressure sabot, then use just the base over the powder charge to protect the sabot and bullet from the higher pressures of smokeless powders.

One of the best and easiest to use sub-bases for the .50 caliber Savage rifle has been the obturator cup (gas seal) cut from the base of a 28-gauge shotgun wad. While the actual "shot cup" of a 28-gauge wad measures approximately .530" in diameter, the base cup or obturator cup actually measures just .001 to .003" over .500". And the soft plastic can be easily compressed by the rifling and slid down the bore of a .50 caliber rifle with very minimal pressure on the ramrod. And once the cup is seated over the powder charge (cup side down), the sabot and bullet can be easily seated over this.

I have used the base cups trimmed from both Winchester "AA" and Claybuster 28-gauge wads to successfully tame the Savage Model 10ML II and a few other .50 caliber in-lines during hot weather. While I usually give the rifles a 5- or 6-minute cool down time, the barrels are still relatively hot. Even so, I've found that the sub-base allows me to keep on shooting and maintaining a high degree of accuracy. If you're having trouble taming down hefty charges of loose-grain Pyrodex RS/Select, Pyrodex "P" or Triple Seven, you may want to try a sub-base. The

Every load must be worked up at the range to ensure that it is a consistent performer. The same care used to load a muzzleloading big game rifle at the range should be used in the field to ensure that same consistency.

best sub-base I've found for a .50 caliber rifle is a base cup trimmed from the rear of a 28-gauge wad. I'm still looking for something that works as well for the .45 caliber bores.

Success with a muzzleloading rifle comes from establishing a good load, then making sure the rifle is loaded the same way each and every time.

Other Tips for Accuracy

Just about every new muzzleloading rifle comes with instructions for proper loading and maintenance. Somewhere in those instructions you're sure to find that for best accuracy with most black powder and Pyrodex loads, the bore should be wiped between shots. This is especially true when loading and shooting a plastic saboted bullet.

When in the field or at the range, I generally moisten a clean cotton patch with a little saliva, and run this down the bore after every shot taken with black powder, Pyrodex or even the cleaner burning Triple Seven. Then I pull the patch back out, flip it over and run it down the bore again.

At that point, the fouling has been reduced to where it will not affect accuracy all that much. In fact, many rifles will shoot better after the first "fouling shot," after the bore has been wiped in this manner. (Most loads fired out of a perfectly spotless bore, will tend to print just a little higher and slightly to one side.)

When shooting the smokeless powder loads in the Savage Model 10ML II, wiping the bore is not absolutely necessary—unless you're trying to obtain a tight 1-inch, 100-yard group. Even smokeless powder leaves a little residue behind, and while it does not build with succeeding shots, this residue can create a variable that will open groups very slightly. A remedy at the range is to run a dry 28-gauge bore-mop down the bore between each and every shot. This wipes away the residue left from each shot, allowing the shooter to shoot with basically a spotless bore each and every time. The bore-mop can be used to wipe the bore after hundreds of shots without cleaning. Soaked in a little nitro solvent for 10 minutes cleans it well enough for use the next time you head for the range.

The consistency of the loads you shoot shouldn't stop while at the range. When you head out on a big game hunt, you should be prepared to load your rifle with the same degree of care if you expect the same level of performance.

Measure your powder charges carefully and carry them in moisture-tight speed loaders. Just about everyone into offering muzzleloader accessories market a speed loader of one sort or another. Some feature short-starters and/or palm savers for slipping over the end of the ramrod to allow consistent seating pressure on the projectile. And most of the loaders now available can accommodate the magnum 150-grain loose-grain or pellet charges.

Before going out after a great buck like this, serious muzzle-loading hunters like Larry Weishuhn take the time to know their rifle and load.

When using the smokeless loads in the Savage rifle, the muzzleloading hunter doesn't really need a loader with such capacity since most of the charges used are 40 to 50 grains. I've found empty .308 Winchester or .30/06 cartridge cases ideal for most charges. I'll weigh my charges on an electronic scale, then use a powder funnel to pour them into the fired case. The case is then sealed with a tiny plastic cap that can be ordered from Brownell's (Montezuma, Iowa) that's used for slipping into the end of a ⅜-inch plastic parts tube offered by the gunsmith supplier. The cap fits perfectly over the neck of a .30 caliber cartridge case. I then use an inch or so piece of vinyl electrician's tape to really seal the case by wrapping it around the lip of the cap and the neck of the brass cartridge. I've kept loads in these for a year without any loss of performance.

When seating the bullet over the powder charge while in the field, try very hard to do so with the same amount of seating pressure used when developing the load and sighting in the rifle. This can be a little difficult if you used an auxiliary ramrod with a nice handle while at the range, then rely on the rifle's shorter ramrod in the field. An easy way to get close is to use a palm saver. This can be fashioned from just about anything into which you can drill a shallow hole into which one end of your ramrod will fit. I've used a short 4-inch-long piece of deer antler to make a very nice palm saver, and have seen others made from just about everything from a small block of oak to a billiard ball. There are even replacement ramrods available for most muzzleloading rifle models that feature an attachment at one end that can swivel to form a T-handle.

Again, always remember that consistency has it rewards. If you can duplicate in the field the load and the loading techniques used to punch those impressive 100-yard groups at the range, you're probably going to be just as impressed with the performance of your muzzleloading big game rifle when you take that shot at the buck or bull of a lifetime.

Compared to the standard No. 11 percussion cap, No. 209 shotshell primers are extremely hot. Most are also sealed and are completely waterproof.

To load sharp-pointed bullets like the Precision Rifle bullets or Hornady SST requires that the tip of the ramrod be drilled out or fitted with a seating adapter.

These empty .30/06 cases are ideal for packing premeasured charges of smokeless powder for the Savage Model 10ML II. A simple plastic cap and a short piece of electrician's tape wrapped around the cap and case make the container extremely waterproof.

When loading and shooting saboted bullets, hot loads in hot weather don't go together. Blown sabots such as these indicate that the plastic material is not withstanding the pressure of the load. When you find sabots similar to this, you're not going to get optimum accuracy.

The gas seal, or obturator cup, cut from the base of a 28-gauge shotgun wad can make an excellent sub-base for .50 caliber rifles when shooting in hot weather or with magnum powder charges. And they are cheap!

coping with
MUZZLELOADER TRAJECTORY

Thanks to improved primer ignition, better-performing powders and the latest in saboted bullets, today's advanced in-line ignition muzzle-loaded big game rifles will shoot faster…flatter…and harder than front-loading rifles of just several decades ago. And when time is taken to precisely match the loading components to the rifle's bore, these muzzleloaders are now fully capable of producing minute-of-angle accuracy.

No muzzleloading rifle manufacturer wants to market a big game rifle that cannot live up to the performance today's hunter has come to expect. Consequently, many of these makers are now making some pretty outlandish claims about the effective game-taking range of these not-so-old-fashioned front-loaders. So, just what is the maximum effective range of today's newer high performance muzzleloading rifles and loads? At what point is the shot "too far"? Well, the answer, for most of us anyway, lies as much in the trajectory of the rifle and load as with the remaining bullet energy at extended ranges.

In other words, the amount of bullet drop out at 150…200…or 250 yards becomes a major limiting factor in taking game with any of today's hotter performing in-line rifles at those distances. What kind of drop can a shooter expect with even maximum loads once the range approaches or surpasses 200 yards? More than the vast majority of muzzleloading hunters realize.

A few winters back, I conducted extensive shooting at 100, 200 and even 300 yards to determine bullet drop with high performance saboted bullet loads. Out of most primer ignition .50 caliber rifles, such as the Thompson/Center Encore 209x50 Magnum, Knight D.I.S.C. Rifle or the Savage Model 10ML II, two 50-grain Pyrodex Pellets loaded with a saboted 250-grain jacketed hollow-point bullet like the Hornady .452 XTP will produce a muzzle velocity of around 1,650 f.p.s. Sighted to hit "dead on" at 100 yards, the bullet would impact the target, on the average, right at 6.3 inches low at 150 yards. At 200 yards, the load would print a full 19 inches down on the target paper, while at 250 yards the bullet would be 49 inches below point of aim. And all the way out at 300 yards, the amount of drop would be an amazing 83 inches low.

Ballistically, this load is effective for game such as white-tailed deer at about a 175-yard maximum. The 250-grain bullet exits the muzzle at about 1,650 f.p.s., with just over 1,500 ft. lbs. of energy. At 150 yards, the amount of knockdown power has diminished to slightly under 1,000 f.p.e., and by the time that bullet gets to 200 yards, it has slowed to around 1,100 f.p.s. and hits with less than 700 foot-pounds of knockdown energy. At that distance, it becomes questionable whether the load will consistently deliver enough energy to cleanly harvest a good buck.

When any of the 22- to 26-inch barreled in-line .50 caliber rifles are loaded with a three 50-grain Pyrodex Pellet charge (150-grain load) behind the same hollow-point bullet, muzzle velocity jumps to right at 2,000 f.p.s. This translates into around 2,200 foot-pounds of muzzle energy. At 100 yards, the 250-grain Hornady XTP would smack a whitetail with around 1,450 f.p.e., and with slightly more than 900 f.p.e. at 200 yards. All the way out to 300 yards, this load would still be good for around 650 foot-pounds of punch—about what the 100-grain Pyrodex Pellet load retained at 200 yards.

The author capitalized on a hunting partner's 225-yard miss on this book class caribou. When the other hunter's shot went under the bull, Bridges put the right amount of elevation on his hold and dropped the trophy bull.

Energy wise, a 150-grain Pyrodex Pellet charge and saboted 250-grain XTP hollow-point can be considered an effective load on deer-sized game to around 200 yards. After that, energy levels really begin to drop. However, when shooting the big jacketed hollow-point bullets, the amount of bullet drop becomes an equally important part of the long-range muzzleloading equation, and may limit the ability of many shooters to accurately place that bullet where it must go on a 200-yard whitetail.

Zeroed to be dead on at 100 yards, the 250-grain Hornady XTP that leaves the muzzle at around 2,000 f.p.s. will hit the target just 4.1 inches low at 150-yards. At 200 yards, this load impacts right at 11 inches below point of aim, and by the time it gets to 250 yards the bullet has dropped 26.5 inches. When it reaches the 300-yard mark, the 250-grain projectile hits 59 inches low.

Perhaps the biggest downfall of the jacketed hollow-point bullets most in-line rifle shooters have been hunting with for much of the past 15 to 20 years is that the blunt-nosed designs result in very poor aerodynamics. The 250-grain Hornady bullet used during the aforementioned trajectory testing has a ballistic coefficient of .147, which means that it has the aerodynamics of a flying ashtray. The design of this bullet may encourage good expansion on game, but also means that the bullet will lose velocity quickly, resulting in excessive drop at longer ranges.

During the spring of 2003, Hornady Manufacturing began production of a brand-new high performance muzzle-loaded big game hunting projectile they've dubbed the SST (Super Shock Tip). Here is a very sleek, very aerodynamic bullet built with many of the same features as Hornady's bullets for loading into center-fire rifle cartridges, including a sharp polymer (plastic) spire-point tip that helps to greatly improve the ballistic coefficient of the SST. In fact, the 250-grain .452" SST sports a b.c. of right at .240. So, what does this higher ballistic coefficient mean to today's performance-minded muzzleloading hunter?

The dramatically improved frontal shape of this bullet offers several advantages over big hollow-pointed pistol bullets. First, the design cuts through the air with less resistance, allowing this bullet to better maintain velocity. Second, with faster downrange velocities comes a decrease in the amount of bullet drop. And third, with the retained velocity also comes higher retained energy levels for greater knockdown power.

One of the hottest smokeless powder loads I've shot from the Savage 10ML II has been 44.5 grains of VihtaVuori N110 topped with a saboted 250-grain bullet. At the muzzle of a 24-inch barrel, this load produces a velocity of 2,368 f.p.s. and generates just over 3,100 f.p.e. These muzzle ballistics are the same whether the rifle is loaded with a 250-grain .452 Hornady XTP hollow-point or a 250-grain spire-pointed .452 Hornady SST.

Even at this high velocity, the hollow-point bullet continues to exhibit considerable drop. Although the XTP bullet drops just 2.6 inches from 100 to 150 yards, it's down more than 9 inches at 200 yards, and drops some 19.5 inches at 250 yards. By comparison, the sleeker 250-grain SST that left the muzzle at the same 2,368 f.p.s. velocity drops just 1.75 inches at 150 yards, impacts just 5.75 inches low at 200 yards, and is still within a foot of point of aim at 250 yards. At 200 yards, the velocity of the 250-grain XTP has slowed to around 1,375 f.p.s., retaining about 1,100 f.p.e. On the other hand, at that distance, the spire-pointed SST is still moving at almost 1,700 f.p.s. and will hit its target with more than 1,600 foot-pounds of whitetail-taking energy.

It takes both velocity and good bullet aerodynamics to maintain a relatively flat trajectory with any of today's modern big game muzzleloaders. Sacrifice one or the other and the result will be a more pronounced rainbow trajectory. As difficult as it may be to accept, actual bullet weight is not the major factor in bullet drop.

Hornady also offers the copper-jacketed SST in a 300-grain version as well. This big .452 diameter polymer-tipped spire-point bullet has a ballistic coefficient of around .290. Shot out of the Savage Model 10ML II with 44.5 grains of VihtaVuori N110, the bullet is good for 2,244 f.p.s. at the muzzle, with an astounding 3,360 f.p.e. Thanks to the high b.c. of this bullet, it is still moving along at almost 1,700 f.p.s. at 200 yards, driving home with more than 1,900 f.p.e. The high b.c. of this bullet also means that due to the exceptional retention of velocity, this bullet drops just 8.5 inches from 100 to 200 yards. That's actually a half–inch

Well-known outdoor writer Tom McIntyre has his Knight in-line rifle sighted to hit "dead on" at 100 yards. Using a near the top of the shoulder hold on this fine near 16-inch pronghorn buck, he cleanly dropped the animal at about 180 yards.

In cover like this, most shots will be within 100 yards, and with today's modern in-line rifles and loads, bullet drop should not be a concern at those distances. But what about when the range extends out to 150…175…or 200 yards?

less drop than the 250-grain XTP hollow-point that was shot from the same rifle at 2,368 f.p.s.

Precision Rifle Custom Muzzleloader Bullets of Manitoba, Canada, currently produces polymer-tipped cold swaged lead bullets with some of the highest ballistic coefficients possible with a muzzle-loaded saboted projectile. The company's saboted 300-grain .45 caliber bullet (for shooting from a .50 or .54 caliber fast-twist bore) has an exceptionally high .376 b.c., which is possibly the highest of any bullet for a .50 caliber bore. A 100-grain charge of FFFg Triple Seven will get this bullet out of a 24-inch barrel at around 1,750 f.p.s. (Hodgdon ballistics), with just over 2,000 f.p.e. The same powder charge propels a 300-grain .452 XTP at the same velocity and with the same energy level. However, the latter is a big jacketed hollow-point with a ballistic coefficient of just .181. With this load, the bullet would retain 1,125 f.p.e. at 200 yards, while the much sleeker and considerably higher .376 b.c. Dead Center bullet that left the muzzle at the same velocity would retain a whopping 1,704 f.p.e.

At 200 yards, the 300-grain XTP that left the muzzle at 2,000 f.p.s. will have slowed to just over 1,300 f.p.s., while the 300-grain Dead Center will still be flying at around 1,600 f.p.s. That added 300 f.p.s. of retained velocity translates into flatter trajectory as well. This load with the big XTP drops 13.75 inches at 200 yards, while the Dead Center prints just over 9 inches down from point of aim.

The author commonly sights his muzzleloading big game rifles an inch or two high at 100 yards, which will permit a "center hold" on just about any whitetail out to about 150 yards, provided the bullet leaves the muzzle at around 2,000 f.p.s. or faster. A bullet that strikes an inch or two high or low from the center of the chest cavity will still take out vital organs. Most deer are shot well within the capabilities of such a "dead on" hold. A rifle so sighted takes guesswork out of making the shot.

When I am faced with stretching a shot to 200 or 225 yards, I rely on experience gained by shooting at those distances to determine the amount of holdover. Generally speaking, using any muzzleloading charge that propels 250- to 300-grain bullets at about 2,000 f.p.s. means simply laying the horizontal crosshair along the back of a deer at 200 yards, then allowing just an inch or two of daylight between the reticle and the animal's back. If the load drops anywhere from 9 to 14 inches, the bullet should still solidly strike the heart and lung area. If the bullet maintains enough energy at that distance, that deer should be laying there when the smoke clears.

For an excellent shot, hunting with a tack-driving in-line rifle loaded with the hottest possible load, a successful 200-yard shot at deer-sized game with a muzzleloader is still something to brag about. Even if the bragging is about the effort that went into the development of the load and shooting to determine long-range trajectory. Some of the hotter loads discussed here are fully capable of delivering a high ballistic coefficient bullet with the accuracy and energy needed to cleanly take game out to 300 yards. Unfortunately, most of us are not.

The information provided in this chapter will give you some idea of what you're up against once you decide to take that "long shot." If you've never checked your rifle and load out on 200-yard target paper, you really don't have any business attempting a 200-yard shot on big game. In the following chapter, this book will take a look at popular scopes and mounting systems that will help to fully tap the downrange performance of your modern high performance muzzleloader.

SCOPING
the high performance muzzleloader

A top-quality high performance muzzleloading big game rifle isn't quite complete unless a good scope has been mounted on the rifle. Today's rifles are fully capable of shooting minute-of-angle accuracy when time is taken to find the right powder and projectile combination for a particular rifle. And to tap that kind of performance, where legal, muzzleloading hunters are abandoning open sights in favor of quality optics on these rifles.

BELOW: When hunting on a frosty morning like this, a quality scope will remain clear and crisp. Remember, good optics are an investment, not an expense.

When the Knight MK-85 was introduced during the mid-1980s, telescopic sights were allowed during the special muzzleloading seasons in fewer than 20 states. Since, one state after another has given into the wishes of hunters looking for more precise shot placement, and as this book was written, 37 or 38 states allowed the use of optics on a front-loaded rifle. And in a few of the others that don't allow all to use a scope, special provisions are made for those with sight impairment to allow the use of optical sights.

For the most part, once a state allows the use of a scope, few restrictions are usually imposed outlining what kind of scope a big game hunter can install on his or her muzzleloader. But unfortunately, there are still a couple states who just can't seem to relinquish control and give into intelligent decision making. Two immediately come to mind: Nebraska and Utah, where hunters may use optical sights…but cannot use a scope with any magnification at all. Sounds ridiculous doesn't it?

The late muzzleloading season in Nebraska is one of the author's favorite muzzleloading hunts for deer. The season now runs the entire month of December, giving residents a great deal of flexibility when trying to steal a day here or a day there to hunt before Christmas or New Years. And the nonresident looking for another great hunt isn't strapped with a narrow window of opportunity. Best of all, permits can be purchased right across the counter at any regional Nebraska Game and Parks office.

In much of the open country in the West, the average shot may be 150 to 200 yards, well beyond the open-sights capability of most hunters today.

Now, if you have ever driven across Nebraska, the first thing you'll notice is the openness of this state, the western two-thirds of it anyway. And an eastern whitetail hunter will quickly wonder how anyone gets within 100 yards of a whitetail. If there was ever a state where a scope with magnifying optics made any sense at all, it would be in Nebraska. One top ranking game department official tried to defend the goofy 1x scope requirement there by claiming it was to keep hunters from attempting long-range shots. This is the same illogic logic imposed by the Utah game department, where shots could stretch 100…150…or 200 yards across an open meadow or narrow canyon.

How a game department can figure that they can control the range of shots taken by hunters through power restrictions on scopes allowed is beyond this hunter. That's the same as trying to dictate ethics. Most hunters who have hunted hard for four or five days, especially during adverse weather conditions, and finally get a nice buck or bull in their sights or scope are going to take a shot—whether the animal is 75…100…125…150…or 175 yards away. Who is most likely to put that shot exactly where it needs to go…the hunter who is mandated by law to hunt with open sights or a non-magnifying "Red Dot" or 1x scope…or the hunter who can install a scope with the magnification to position the reticle exactly on the target where the projectile needs to hit for a clean, efficient and humane kill?

Wound loss during the special muzzleloading seasons is primarily not because of the ineffectiveness of the load that's being hunted with. Big game animals that are lost during these seasons or hunts are largely lost due to the ineffective muzzleloading regulations in place in a state. Regulations that dictate the use of a rifle, powder, projectile and sighting system that is less than ideal are not in the best interest of muzzleloader hunting. If a game department must control the number of a big game species taken during the special muzzleloader seasons, they need to do so through permit quotas, not through hampering the hunter's ability to do the best job possible when a shot is taken. The latter route is the unethical route, resulting in more lost animals than most game departments realize.

TOP: In thick cover, a scope of high magnification is definitely a handicap. However, a good 3-9x variable allows a hunter to turn down the magnification when hunting thick brush, then turn it back up once back in the open.

BOTTOM: Precise shot placement in cover like this is much easier when the high performance muzzleloading rifle is fitted with a properly sighted scope.

Choosing a Scope

I can't think of a single current production in-line ignition muzzleloader that does not come pre-drilled and tapped for scope base installation. Installing a scope on a muzzle-loaded big game rifle has never been easier. And anyone with a little patience and a screwdriver or an Allen wrench set can take a new rifle…a new scope base…a new set of rings…and a new scope and have the scoped muzzleloader ready to head for the range in 30 minutes or less.

The only bits of advice I can give about choosing a scope for any of today's

When selecting a scope for a muzzleloading big game rifle, always pay close attention to the amount of eye relief the scope offers. Get too close to the rear of the scope and you're going to get bitten!

top performing frontloaded hunting rifles are: 1. Buy the best quality scope you can afford. It's an investment in accuracy and dependability, not an expense. 2. Do not choose a scope with less than a 3-inch eye relief. Muzzleloaders have longer recoil than a modern center-fire rifle. Get too close to the rear lens of a scope, and you could go home with a nasty cut above your eye. This is especially true when shooting really heavy powder charges behind a heavy bullet. If you can find a model with 3½ to 4 inches of eye relief, you'll be a lot safer. 3. Forget that you're shooting a muzzle-loaded rifle. Too often, shooters under scope their muzzleloaders, convincing themselves that it is only a short-range hunting rig, when in actuality the majority of today's modern in-line rifles stuffed with an optimum load are true 200-yard big game rifles. So, scope it like the big game rifle it really is. Don't settle for just a 2.5- or 4-power scope, unless that's exactly what you want.

The majority of modern in-line rifles that are scoped are usually topped with a 3-9x scope with at least a 40mm front objective lens. In fact, quite a few muzzleloading rifle manufacturers offer complete package rigs that come with rifle, scope already mounted, and just about everything a shooter would need to pull that rifle from the packaging and begin shooting.

Most of these come with a variable scope of 3 to 9 power. A scope with this range of magnification offers a great deal of flexibility. At the lowest 3x setting, the rifle becomes a great woods rifle, allowing the hunter to quickly find game, even in relatively thick cover. Then, when the magnification is turned up to 9x, and the rifle has been properly sighted in, it becomes a more effective open country rifle. Targets at 100 to 200 yards appear much larger, allowing a more precise hold on where the bullet is to hit.

Hunters who settle for a scope of much lower magnification may never ever discover the degree of accuracy their rifle and load are fully capable of producing. A standard crosshair reticle can cover a lot of the target when viewed through a low-power magnification scope of 2.5x or 4x, making very precise aiming impossible. The same target viewed through 9x magnification will permit the shooter to refine his or her hold on a larger target. And the more precise that aim is, the tighter the groups with a good load.

Since many of the higher performance muzzle-loaded rifles, like the T/C Encore 209x50 Magnum, Savage Model 10ML II and Knight D.I.S.C. Extreme, can now shoot right along with most quality center-fire rifles at 100 yards, and experience minimum drop out to 200 yards, more and more shooters are now installing still higher magnification scopes on these rifles. It is now not uncommon to see 4-12x scopes on many of these rifles, better harnessing their 200+-yard effectiveness.

Several seasons back, I was doing a lot of testing of new spire-pointed muzzleloader hunting projectiles, and to help reduce human error when sighting, I mounted one of the big 6-18x 50mm Leatherwood/Hi-Lux Optics upper end scopes on one of my Savage Model 10ML II .50 caliber rifles. With the right loads of smokeless powder in this rifle, I could push these bullets at maximum velocities (2,300+ f.p.s.) and found several to print near one-hole groups at 100 yards, and often kept 200-yard groups inside of 2 inches.

My intentions were to take the big scope off come hunting season and use the same rifle and most accurate load for a Missouri late muzzleloader hunt for whitetails. But, I had that rig shooting so well, I just couldn't force myself to loosen and remove that big target-varmint scope. Opening morning of the hunt found me sitting in a climbing tree stand nearly 40 feet off the ground, watching a near constant parade of whitetails work through the heavy brush of a small pocket I could watch from my lofty perch. About 8 o'clock that morning a doe suddenly came running into the pocket, kicking up a cloud of freshly fallen snow. I didn't need to watch her for long to determine what was up. I knew a buck would be close behind, so I reached up and lifted my rifle from the screw-in step I had turned into the tree trunk. I had just slipped off the protective lens covers when a beautiful 200+ -pound 11-pointer came following the same course taken by the doe.

The scope had been turned down to 6x, but I still had one heck of a time keeping up with the buck as he darted in and out of the heavy cover 150 yards away. Fortuantely, the deer stopped for a few seconds in a small opening, and I was able to get the crosshairs on his shoulder just as he started to step out. The trigger came back and the rifle bucked rearward lightly as the smokeless load fired. The bullet found its mark and that buck now hangs on my office wall. After the difficulty I had in finding the buck running in and out of the thick brush, I decided right then and there to never hunt again with any scope having a minimum power greater than 4x.

Specialized Muzzleloader Scopes

Twenty years ago when anyone talked of a "muzzleloader scope," they were referring to one of the long brass-tube scopes of low power that were used during the mid-1800s, or a modern reproduction of those scopes.

Yes, telescopic sights have been around that long, and longer. In fact, scopes have been in use longer than many of the so-called side-hammer percussion rifle designs many traditional-minded muzzleloading shooters hold in high esteem as being of authentic muzzleloading design. (Maybe someone needs to get this across to those stubborn game departments who cling to "no scope" regulations!)

Today there are several manufacturers

The center-fire rifle toting big game hunter headed for open country such as this would never think of doing so without a good scope on his rifle. And neither should you.

who specifically market a muzzleloader scope of modern optics design. For the most part, these have basically been built to better withstand the long recoil of muzzleloading guns. Keep in mind, that when the powder is ignited in a modern center-fire cartridge rifle, the smokeless powder load is mostly burnt in about half the length of the bore. Consequently, recoil may be a little on the sharp side, but short in nature. On the other hand, it takes all of the bore to completely burn the heavy 100- to 150-grain charges of black powder, Pyrodex or Triple Seven now recommended by so many in-line rifle makers. And due to the longer burn of the powder charge, the length of the recoil is longer. And it is tougher on the internal construction of a scope.

Actually, the recoil of a high performance muzzleloading big game rifle is very much like the recoil of a shotgun loaded with slug loads. And any scope that has been built to withstand the pounding of a 12-gauge slug-shooting whitetail shotgun will double nicely for use on the hardest recoiling muzzle-loaded hunting rifle. Unfortuantely, many shotgun scopes don't offer the magnification dis-

The majority of states now permit the use of a scope during the muzzleloading big game seasons. Iowa hunter Todd Lust took this brute whitetail buck during the state's late muzzleloading season, with a scoped Knight in-line .50 caliber rifle.

cussed earlier, and often come with only a 32mm or smaller front objective which could create light gathering problems during the first and last light of the day.

Now, if you're looking for a really first-class muzzleloader scope, Kahles offers several models, including a 3.5-10x 50mm model that features their TDS range-compensating reticle. This is a fancy way of saying that in addition to the primary crosshairs, the scope also features four short crosshairs on the vertical reticle line below the intersection of the horizontal reticle line. This allows a shooter to sight dead on with the primary crosshair, then the rifle can be shot with each of the other lower aiming points (raising point of impact) to determine where they are "on" at extended ranges. Knowing the point of impact at each line could eliminate guessing at ranges of 150...200...and 225 or so yards.

Burris, Sightron, Leatherwood/Hi-Lux Optics and a few other scope suppliers also offer similar arrangements. With some models, the lower aiming points are short crosshairs as well, with others they are dots, often referred to as a mil dot which can be used to help determine range. The Leatherwood No-Math Mil-Dot Models include framing marks on each side of the intersection of the vertical and horizontal crosshairs. This allows the hunter to frame an object of known 18-inch size (like the top to bottom measurement of a whitetail's chest cavity) between these marks, then read right on top of the scope the exact yardage. These scopes also feature the standard mil dots below the crosshairs, giving the muzzleloading hunter secondary long-range aiming points.

Easily, the most advanced muzzleloading scope on the market is another Leatherwood model—the In-Liner. Built with the same Automatic Ranging & Trajectory technology Jim Leatherwood developed for military snipers in Vietnam, the In-Liner literally takes all of the guesswork out of shooting at 100...150...200...250...and 300 yards with just about any bullet shooting muzzleloader and load.

This is accomplished through an external cam, which can be calibrated to compensate for the drop of practically any of today's muzzle-loaded bullets fired at velocities from 1,600 to 2,300 f.p.s. Once the ranging ring and cam have been calibrated to a shooter's load, then the scope is sighted in to print "dead on" at 100 yards; the ranging ring is then turned to any other yardage up to 300 yards and the cam lifts the rear of the scope to compensate for bullet drop. It works amazingly well.

Not many center-fire rifle hunters would even think about going afield with a flat-shooting .270 Winchester or 7mm Remington Magnum big game rifle with just open sights. And neither should the serious muzzleloading big game hunter who has taken the time and made the effort to work up an honest 200-yard load for his front-loader. A good scope makes a lot of sense on any big game hunting rifle—whether it loads from the front or the rear.

Many of today's modern in-line rifles, like the Savage Model 10ML II shown here, are capable of center-fire rifle quality accuracy. A good scope makes as much sense on one of these rifles as on any cartridge taking big game rifle.

MAINTAINING
the muzzle-loaded big game hunting rifle

How many times have you stayed on stand right up until almost dark, then in the last light of evening the buck you've been after magically materializes from out of nowhere, offering you a perfect shot well within range of the rifle and load you're hunting with? You make the shot, and the deer goes down. While a feeling of satisfaction fills your body as you walk out to the downed buck, you also realize that the fun is over. Now the work begins.

Not only must you get that deer field-dressed and out of the woods, in many states the deer must be taken to a check station that very same day. And if the weather is on the warm side, you're faced with either getting the animal skinned and possibly quartered, then into a cooler, or taken to a nearby processing plant. By the time you slow down long enough to eat a bite of dinner, it could be nine to ten o'clock—and you still have a dirty muzzleloader that will require cleaning before you turn in.

Each year, thousands of high quality muzzleloading big game rifles are lost to neglect. The residue left behind by a single shot with a load of black powder or Pyrodex, which contain sulfur, can completely destroy any chances of future accuracy with just about any front-loaded rifle barrel the propellant was fired through. Not only is this residue very corrosive in nature, but also tends to be extremely hygroscopic. In other words, the residue left behind by black powder or Pyrodex will literally pull moisture right out of the air, making the dirty film covering the inside of the bore, and the ignition system, even more corrosive and harmful to the rifle. During damp and very humid weather conditions, the residue left by a single shot can ruin a bore practically overnight!

Of course, the ideal solution is to give that rifle a thorough cleanup before turning in that evening. But, as most of you already know, this isn't always possible. However, there are a few things you can do to buy yourself time until the next day, when you have the time and energy to give your high performance muzzleloading big game rifle the cleaning and attention it deserves.

Preventive Field Maintenance

It takes only a few minutes to wipe the vast majority of fouling from the bore of your rifle. A good habit to get into is to carry a dozen or so cleaning patches with you every time you head into the field. And if the ramrod of your rifle is not fitted

FAR LEFT: When the trigger is pulled on this rifle, a charge of black powder or any of the black powder substitutes will leave behind a damaging coat of fouling in the bore. If not cleaned that same day, the bore could be ruined overnight.

The success of a muzzleloading hunt means the fun is over and the work begins. Not only must the game be field-dressed, gotten out of the field, and often to a check station before the hunter retires that evening but also a dirty muzzleloader needs to be tended to.

with a cleaning jag, then also pack along one of these. The patches and jag can be slipped into a sandwich-sized plastic baggie and carried in a jacket or pants pocket without adding any real weight or bulk to what you already carry afield.

Now, after you've made the shot and you know the game you're hunting has been effectively put down, wipe the bore of the empty rifle with four or five saliva or creek water dampened patches. Black powder and Pyrodex fouling is completely water (and saliva) soluble, meaning that if enough of the stuff is used, the powder residue could be cleaned from the bore with nothing more than water. Two or three dry patches would then remove moisture from the bore, and leave it 80 to 90 percent clean.

Once back in camp, the wise shooter will take a few minutes to break the removable breech plug of an in-line rifle free, maybe even remove it completely. Then the bore and breech plug can be quickly sprayed with a liberal douse of a water-displacing lubricant, such as good ol' WD-40. This not only counters any saliva (or water) left in the bore from wiping it with the dampened patches, but also saturates and coats what little powder fouling that's left in the rifling, preventing it from drawing moisture out of the damp night air.

It takes less than five minutes to wipe fouling from the bore after making a successful shot during a late afternoon or evening hunt, and less than that to break the breech plug loose and spray a protective coat of moisture-displacing lubricant down the bore and on any other fouling covered metal surfaces. This 10 minutes of preventive maintenance will save any high quality muzzle-loaded hunting rifle from the scrap pile, provided the hunter follows up with a complete, thorough cleaning the following day.

Follow-Up Cleaning

Cleaning a dirty muzzleloading rifle is more than likely the "No. 1 Apprehension" among new "would-be" muzzleloading shooters. That's right, it is likely the fear of having to thoroughly clean all of that dirty, corrosive fouling from these rifles within a reasonably short time period after they've been shot, which has kept many new shooters and hunters from coming into the sport. It is also the main reason why, on the average, muzzleloading rifle owners seldom put more than a hundred rounds a year through their front-loaded big game rifles. But, is it really all that much trouble to keep these guns spotless and functioning perfectly?

Many of those shooters who do burn two…three…four or more pounds of black powder or Pyrodex through their muzzleloaders on an annual basis have come to realize that once the rifle is cased, there is a natural tendency to procrastinate with the necessary follow-up cleaning. And for that reason, many carry all of their cleaning gear and cleaning solutions right to the range with them. After shooting the rifle, it is cleaned right there, before it ever finds its way back into the case, on the gun rack or in the gun cabinet.

When at the range, many hunters do their cleaning right at the bench following their last shots. This ensures that the job is done.

With just about every modern in-line on the market, the breech plug can be quickly and easily removed to facilitate cleaning. These rifles come with the necessary breech plug wrench and usually any other tools, such as an Allen wrench, for disassembling the rifle. Most of today's more advanced designs can be totally broken down for a thorough cleaning in just a few minutes, leaving the shooter with only several major component parts for cleaning. Generally speaking, these include the barrel, hammer or bolt, breech plug (and possibly nipple), and trigger assembly.

Following the cleaning instructions provided by each rifle manufacturer, just about any of today's more popular models can be thoroughly cleaned in a matter of 10 to 15 minutes. There are a number of black powder or Pyrodex cleaning solvents that have been formulated to speed up the time it takes to dissolve or break down the residue left behind by these powders, making it easier for the shooter to give his favorite muzzleloader a complete, thorough cleaning right at the range, on the tailgate of his pickup or in hunting camp.

Many muzzleloading shooters come up with their own cleaning solutions, which are generally not much more than dishwashing detergent and water. Even these soapy solutions will speed up the cleaning process and clean black powder or Pyrodex fouling from a rifle's bore and other parts in short order. Plus, such solutions will also break down the greasy film left behind by the heavy lubes used on most bore-sized conical bullets.

For the most part, powder and bullet lube fouling can be completely cleaned from the bore of the barrel with 6 to 10 solvent saturated patches, followed by four or five dry patches, then a lightly lubed patch, again using one of today's advanced moisture-displacing lubricants. While the barrel is being cleaned, veteran shooters regularly let the breech plug, nipple, face of the hammer, or other fouling covered parts of the rifle soak in some of the solution that has been poured into a cup, small bowl or what have you. Then, these can be easily cleaned by scrubbing away the residue, using an old toothbrush, typewriter cleaning brush, or similar small bristle brush. After they have been cleaned free of fouling residue, the parts should be dried and sprayed with lubricant.

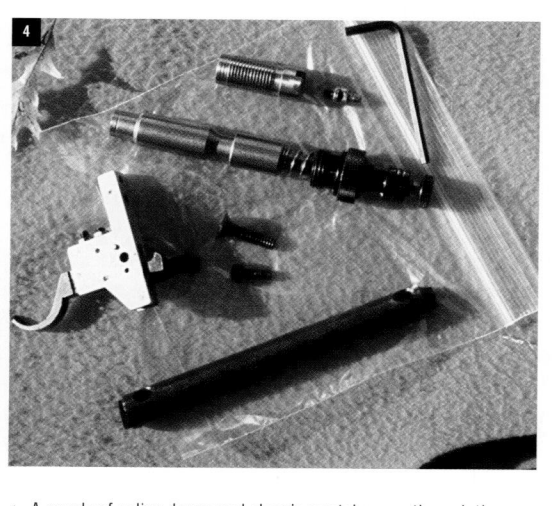

1. A couple of saliva dampened cleaning patches run through the bore after making a shot in the deer woods will remove the vast majority of the fouling left in the bore from one or two shots.

2. The fouling left from a single shot that's left in the bore for a day or longer is enough to completely ruin the barrel of a deadly accurate high performance muzzleloading big game rifle.

3. A small Ziplock plastic bag with a dozen or so cotton cleaning patches and a cleaning jag fits nearly undetected into a jacket or pants pocket, allowing the hunter to give his rifle a quick cleaning right in the field.

4. A simple emergency repair kit such as this could save your entire muzzleloading season. Spare parts such as a complete hammer, trigger or even a few simple screws and nipple aren't always readily available. Having spares before the season or hunt begins offers peace of mind.

5. The smokeless powders shot out of the Savage Model 10ML II, like IMR-4227, are noncorrosive and the minute amount of residue left behind by a dozen or more shots will not harm the rifle's barrel.

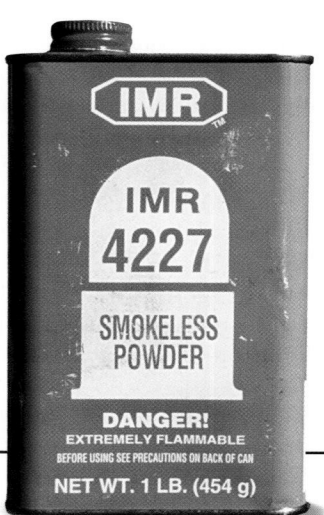

The trigger assembly should never be submerged in cleaning solution. If there is a little fouling on the sear or any other part of the trigger, carefully wipe it away with a lightly solvent dampened patch; dry and lubricate. When applying lube, don't go overboard. A little goes a long way.

When reassembling a modern in-line rifle with a removable breech plug, ALWAYS apply the manufacturer's recommended breech plug grease or lube to the threads of the breech plug. If these are installed without any lube whatsoever, the next time the rifle is fired, the breech plug may prove to be not so removable. While there tends to be some disagreement among the rifle makers over what works best, it seems that those shooters who turn to the automotive anti-seize compounds pretty well unanimously agree that these lubes also make the finest breech plug lubricants as well.

The stainless steel Savage Model 10ML II is as "maintenance free" as muzzleloading is likely ever to get. The cleaning of this rifle can be put off for a day...a week...even a month or longer without causing damage to the bore.

Plastic Fouling in the Barrel

Back when most modern in-line rifle shooters were just beginning to make the switch to loading, shooting and hunting with the plastic saboted jacketed handgun bullets, there was some debate to whether or not the plastic sabots actually left any plastic residue in the bore. Then the most popular powder charge was 90 to 100 grains of Pyrodex "RS/Select." Now that an ever growing number of performance-minded muzzleloading hunters have made the switch to shooting heavier 150-grain powder charges, there is now no doubt that some fouling is left behind by the plastic sabot.

The soapy water solutions, and even the commercially available "black powder" cleaning solvents, do little to combat this fouling. Following a thorough cleaning to remove powder fouling, the shooter who looks to maintain the pinpoint accuracy capable with saboted bullets will want to follow up by running a wire bore brush through the bore 10 to 20 times to break any plastic fouling loose. Several patches saturated with a modern shotgun cleaning solvent should then be run through the bore to remove the loose residue. You'll be amazed at how black these patches will come out of the barrel. Follow up with a couple of dry patches. Then, the last patch through the bore should be lightly oiled.

Cleaning Has Gotten Easier Than Ever!

The Model 10ML II "smokeless powder" muzzleloader from Savage Arms is as "maintenance free" as muzzleloading guns have ever gotten, especially the stainless steel models of this unique front-loader. The fouling left behind by charges of powders like IMR-4227 or VihtaVuori N110, which perform so well in the rifle, is noncorrosive. Another favorable attribute of the smokeless loads for this rifle is

Keeping a high performance muzzleloading big game rifle in top operating and shooting condition in a remote camp requires having the right tools and cleaning products with you.

that the light residue left behind by burning charges does not tend to build and has very little effect of accuracy. This rifle can be shot, then put away for months without being thoroughly cleaned and without worry of ruining the muzzleloader. However, when a shooter knows it will be several days before the rifle can be cleaned, it is still a good idea to break the breech plug loose before putting the rifle away. This simple precaution ensures that the plug remains "removable."

Clean-up of a fired Model 10ML II bore is a snap. Usually, all I do is run two or three cleaning patches through the bore that have been lightly dampened with a top-quality nitro bore solvent, such as the bore cleaner available from Shooter's Choice (Middlefield, Ohio). Then I follow up with a dry patch or two and another with a light application of a good lubricant. After every 100 or so shots through the bore, I find it advisable to run a bronze bore brush through the barrel 10 or so times to make sure there is no plastic residue left from the sabots that travel along the rifling at 2,200 to 2,300 f.p.s. Before reinstalling the breech plug, I'll liberally fill the first three or four threads with a copper- or nickel-based anti-seize. (Due to the much higher heat generated by the smokeless loads in this rifle, do not use standard grease-based breech plug lubes.)

Hodgdon's new Triple Seven black powder substitute somewhat bridges the gap between black powder and smokeless powder. While the powder has been formulated to give optimum velocities from high quality muzzleloading rifles, it is not nitrocellulose based. Unlike black powder or Pyrodex, Triple Seven *does not* include sulfur, which makes the fouling left by the other two muzzleloader propellants extremely smelly during clean-up.

Hodgdon is not making any claims about the noncorrosive nature of Triple Seven, but without sulfur in its chemical makeup, the fouling left behind by burning charges is far less harmful to internal metal surfaces than either black powder or Pyrodex fouling. While Triple Seven fouling does clean up relatively easy with just water, shooters have had two minor complaints about the powder. First, it tends to leave something of a crusty ring in the bore, three or four inches in front of the breech plug. And some shooters have experienced hard-to-remove breech plugs (often impossible to remove). A solution for the latter problem has been to apply a thin piece of plumber's pink Teflon tape to the forward three or four threads of the breech plug before applying the breech plug grease. While the fouling left by burning charges of Triple Seven may not be as corrosive as with some other powders, Hodgdon says the fouling is still somewhat hygroscopic and recommends a thorough cleaning after shooting the powder in any muzzleloader.

Someone once stated that "Cleanliness is next to Godliness!" When it comes to muzzleloading, cleanliness is also mandatory to keep the front-loaders functioning properly and shooting accurately. A top-quality high performance muzzleloading big game rifle represents a major investment. Isn't it worth 10 or 15 minutes of cleaning to keep it shooting with peak performance at the end of a few hours at the range or at the end of a successful day of hunting?

Not only does this caribou bull have to be dressed, skinned, boned and carried back to camp, but the in-line rifle has to be thoroughly cleaned!

muzzleloading
FOR DEER

When the topic of muzzleloading for big game comes up, more than 90 percent of the time the topic is really muzzleloading for white-tailed deer. In the United States, hunters pursue whitetails more than any other big game animal. In fact, more hunters go after this species than all other big game species found on the North American continent combined. So, it stands to reason that these deer which inhabit the northern forests, coastal plains, southern swamps, Midwestern woodlots and cornfields, as well as the scattered pockets of brush all across the plains, are the first choice of the muzzleloading hunter as well.

Due to the wide range of terrain and cover the whitetail can be found inhabiting, the criteria for an "adequate" muzzle-loaded rifle and load for these deer can vary from region to region. This is due largely to how greatly these deer can vary in size, and the typical distance at which most are taken. A 400-pound live weight buck out on the plains of Saskatchewan will require more knockdown power than a southern Alabama buck that might not top 150 pounds live weight —soaking wet! Likewise, the hunter in the open farm country of the Midwest may find it necessary to stretch a shot out to and slightly past 200 yards, while the hunter looking to get a shot in heavy forest or thick swamp may find getting a shot much past 50 to 75 yards extremely rare.

For many years, modern cartridge firearm deer hunting experts have established the maximum effective range of a given caliber rifle on deer-sized game to be at the distance where the bullet began to hit with any less than 1,000 foot-pounds of energy. For the most part, we're talking about center-fire cartridges ranging between .24 to .35 caliber, with only a few .44 and larger bore sizes thrown in. Calibers like the .243 Winchester, .25/06 Remington, .270 Winchester, 7mm Remington Magnum, .30/30 Winchester, .30/06 Springfield and the .35 Remington are generally loaded with bullets ranging from around 100 to 250 grains.

In most states, muzzleloaders of .45 caliber on up are legal for use on whitetailed deer, with the .50 caliber rifles most widely used. The larger frontal mass of the larger diameter projectiles used in these guns do add another element to their terminal performance on game. Still, the maximum effective range of the muzzle-loading deer rifle is also pretty much governed by the amount of retained energy of the load shot. A good rule of thumb would be around 900 f.p.e. to ensure a quick clean harvest.

The lightest projectile available for the .45 caliber bore is the patched round

FAR LEFT: Knowledgeable muzzleloading deer hunters, like hunting video producer Mark Drury, shoot the hardest-hitting and most accurate load possible from the muzzleloader they hunt with. When a buck like this shows up, they leave nothing to chance.

Today's muzzleloading deer hunter cares less about the nostalgia of muzzleloading. They are serious hunters looking to shoot the most effective rifle and load possible.

In many parts of the South, even a big buck might be lucky to tip the scales at 150 pounds live weight. Loads can be more moderate and still cleanly harvest any deer shot at within the effective range of the load.

ball, which would commonly range from around 128 grains (.440" ball) to 133 grains (.445" ball). Shot from a 28-inch barreled Thompson/Center Arms "Hawken" rifle with a 90-grain charge of FFFg black powder, the load would have a muzzle velocity of around 2,100 f.p.s., with 1,300 f.p.e. Due to the poor aerodynamics of the round ball, this speedster would drop to around 1,700 f.p.s. at about 50 yards, and hit with just 850 f.p.e. And by the time that ball reached 100 yards, it would be moving at only about 1,100 f.p.s. and retain less than 400 f.p.e. In short, this load is, at best, an effective 50-yard load for whitetails.

The same rifle loaded with a 240-grain T/C "Maxi-Ball" and 90 grains of FFg black powder is good for 1,600 f.p.s. at the muzzle, and 1,360 f.p.e. However, since this bullet is more aerodynamic and heavier than the ball, it retains velocity and energy much better. Out at 100 yards, this load is still good for close to 1,300 f.p.s. and 900 f.p.e., making it an effective load for whitetails and other similar-sized big game at that distance.

One of Hornady's 200-grain SST polymer-tipped spire-pointed .40 caliber bullets loaded with a sabot into a 26-inch barreled in-line rifle like the Thompson/Center Arms Encore 209x45 Super Magnum with a 100-grain charge of FFFg Triple Seven will leave the muzzle at around 2,250 f.p.s. The load develops right at 2,250 f.p.e. at the muzzle. Thanks to the vastly improved aerodynamics of this bullet and high .225 ballistic coefficient, this bullet is still good for more than 1,100 foot-pounds of knockdown power all the way out at 200 yards. So loaded, one of today's hot .45s is still a great choice for shots at deer at that distance—and a few yards farther.

The .50 caliber has been the favorite of muzzleloading deer hunters now for more than 30 years. It has proven to be the most versatile of all muzzleloading big game rifles, with a tremendous range of projectile designs and weight available for the bore size.

For comparison with the .45, we'll start with the round ball loads that were popular through the early 1970s. Loaded with a 100-grain charge of FFFg black powder, a patched 178-grain .490" soft lead ball will be pushed from the muzzle of a .50 caliber 28-inch barreled T/C Hawken at about 1,875 f.p.s., generating about 1,400 f.p.e. At 50 yards, the velocity of the load has diminished to around 1,550 f.p.s. and hits with around 975 f.p.e. At about 60 yards, the ball will dip below 900 foot-pounds in retained energy. And when the 178-grain sphere reaches 100 yards, speed has dropped to around 1,150 f.p.s. Likewise, retained energy is down to 477 foot-pounds of punch. The maximum effective range of this load is between 60 and 65 yards.

Stuffed with a 370-grain "Maxi-Ball" conical and 90 grains of FFg black

Jacketed hollow-point bullets like the 250-grain Hornady .452" XTP, loaded into a muzzleloader with a plastic sabot, have become the most widely used muzzleloader hunting projectiles wherever whitetails are hunted.

powder, the 28-inch barreled Hawken spits the bullet out of the muzzle just under 1,500 f.p.s., with almost 1,800 f.p.e. At 100 yards, the big conical would still hit a whitetail with around 1,150 f.p.e. At about 130 yards, the big bullet would drop below the 900 foot-pound mark.

Loaded with three Triple Seven pellets (150-grain equivalent load) behind a saboted 250-grain Hornady SST polymer-tipped spire-point bullet, one of Knight's 26-inch barreled .50 caliber D.I.S.C. Extreme models will get this bullet out of the muzzle at around 2,025 f.p.s. The load generates 2,275 f.p.e. At 100 yards, the .240 b.c. bullet will retain 1,950 foot-pounds of punch, and at 200 yards smacks a big ol' whitetail buck with right at 1,250 foot-pounds of knockdown power.

With conical bullet loads the .54 caliber rifles can show an edge over the .50 caliber when loaded with the same design bullet. However, most saboted loads shot out of the majority of .54 caliber rifles utilize the same .429" and .451"/.452" bullets shot out of the .50 caliber bores. The slightly larger diameter of the .54 bore often means that an additional 10 or so grains of powder can be consumed for a slight increase in velocity. However, the trade-off is very often poorer accuracy due to the heavier plastic surrounding the bullet. An exception to the accuracy rule can be some of the .50 caliber bullets shot with a sabot out of a .54 bore. Since these are much closer to actual bore size, accuracy can be great. One such bullet for the .54 is the 275-grain Barnes all-copper Expander MZ. With a 120-grain charge of FFg Triple Seven, the load is good for just over 1,700 f.p.s., with 1,760 f.p.e. This bullet has a .184 ballistic coefficient, which means it slows to around 1,400 f.p.s. at 100 yards, retaining right at 1,200 f.p.e. At 200 yards, veloc-

The dramatically improved aerodynamics (and higher ballistic coefficient) of new bullet designs, like the Hornady SST shown above the Hornady Lock-N-Load Speed sabot, maintain velocity and retain longer range than older saboted hollow-point bullets.

The author's smokeless powder Savage Model 10ML II is fully capable of delivering performance levels that surpass older favorite deer rifles as the .30/30 Winchester, .35 Remington and even the .35 Whelen.

ity with this load is down to around 1,100 f.p.s., meaning the 275-grain all-copper hollow-point hits with only about 750 f.p.e. I'd limit shots with this one to around 175 yards.

The hottest shooting muzzleloader out there today is the Savage Model 10ML II. This .50 caliber gets all of its zip and punch from the smokeless loads it can digest. I've gotten the saboted 250-grain Hornady SST out of the muzzle at 2,437 f.p.s. with a 46-grain charge of VihtaVuori N110. Now, this load develops an amazing 3,290 f.p.e. At 100 yards, the bullet is still zipping along at around 2,050 f.p.s. with 2,335 f.p.e. And at 200 yards, the load is still good for 1,750 f.p.s. and 1,700 foot-pounds of wallop. Furthermore, the load still hits with around 1,200 f.p.e. all the way out at 300 yards! There's still plenty of knockdown power left in this one at that distance, a shooter just has to learn how to cope with the more than two feet of drop—and better be darn good at estimating range. Or…carry a laser rangefinder with him.

Many of you reading this may favor heavier or lighter bullets than those covered here. Over the years, I have taken more than 250 whitetails with muzzle-loaded rifles in calibers ranging from .45 up to .58, and with projectiles ranging from a light 128-grain .440" round ball to a huge 600-grain .58 caliber hollow-based Minié bullet. Easily 90 percent of the deer I have taken with a muzzleloader have been shot with a .50 caliber. And probably 90 percent of those have been harvested with saboted bullets of 240 to 260 grains. Personally, I have found bullets of that weight ideal for any game in the 200- to 300-pound class. An old favorite has been the 250-grain .452" Hornady XTP jacketed hollow-point, a new favorite is the Hornady SST polymer-tipped .452" spire-point bullet.

While on a muzzleloading pronghorn hunt with my good friend Jim Shockey a few years ago, I helped him sight in his favorite .50 caliber Knight MK-85 with the 300-grain Barnes Expander MZ he intended to use for that hunt, and

The same loads that work well for hunting open country whitetails will double nicely for most pronghorn hunting.

Big mule deer at 200 yards can be tough to put down, requiring the hunter to work up a load that shoots accurately at such distances, delivers the punch needed and which does not have the trajectory of a thrown brick!

Muzzleloading hunter Bruce Watley with a fine cornfield buck. Today's modern muzzle-loaded rifles and loads not only make those 200-yard shots possible, but practical as well.

all of his other hunts that fall. He intended to use the same bullet on everything, from pronghorns to grizzlys. When I asked him why he needed such a big bullet for whitetails, he said he didn't really feel that he needed it, he just wanted to shoot the same bullet and the same load for everything he hunted that fall. And that he would much rather over kill a whitetail than under kill a grizzly. I couldn't argue with his way of thinking.

going after
BIGGER GAME

In the previous chapter, this book took a look at loads with various types of projectiles that should perform adequately on big game the size of the white-tailed deer, provided the hunter knows the range limitations of his rifle and load. Now, the average live weight of a mature whitetail buck will probably average just a little over 200 pounds from north to south, east to west. Any load capable of maintaining 900 to 1,000 foot-pounds of energy at the distance of the shot should deal a lethal blow, as long as the rifle, powder charge and projectile combination is accurate enough to place that shot exactly where it needs to hit—right in the vitals.

But what about hunting game that can be two…three…four…five or more times larger than your standard issue whitetail deer? What calibers are best suited? How heavy must the projectile be to ensure penetration? What kind of powder charge is needed to get enough velocity to develop massive amounts of energy? And at what point is the distance too far to chance a shot?

Strange as it may sound, many hunters use some of the same loads that deliver outstanding performance for deer-sized game to also harvest elk, caribou, bear, moose and other game that can weigh from 400 to more than 1,000 pounds on the hoof—or paw. However, here we're not talking about the "iffy" round ball loads a few purists feel compelled to use on such larger game, but instead the harder-hitting saboted and bore-sized conical bullets that cross over into the realm of high performance muzzleloading.

The first elk I ever took with a muzzleloader was during the general firearms elk season in Colorado during the mid-1970s. I was hunting with a custom full-stocked Leman .50 caliber rifle I had built myself, which turned out pretty damned nice if I must say so myself. I was so proud of that rifle, I hunted everything with it for a couple of seasons, shooting a 110-grain charge of FFg black powder behind a tightly patched 180-grain .495" soft lead ball. At the muzzle of the 32-inch Douglas barrel, the load was good for 2,065 f.p.s., with 1,700 foot-pounds of energy.

The first season with the rifle and load, I dumped a half-dozen whitetails at ranges up to about 110 yards, several wild hogs and a dandy 350-pound black bear as it fed on a bait 35 yards away from my stand. I was so sure of the rifle's killing power, it was a logical choice, or so I thought, for my first elk hunt early the next fall. And I hunted confidently with the rifle thrown over my shoulder for

FAR LEFT: William "Tony" Knight relied on a 110-grain charge of Pyrodex "RS/Select" behind a huge saboted 325-grain .50 caliber Speer jacketed hollow-point to deliver the lethal blow to this 500+ - pound black bear. He was shooting a .54 caliber Knight in-line rifle.

The author with more than 1,200 pounds of moose, brought down by a single saboted 300-grain Hornady .452" XTP and 110 grains of Pyrodex RS/Select. The bull went just 60 yards before going down after being shot with the .50 caliber Knight MK-85.

four days before slipping up on a bedded 5x5 that was all alone in a thicket near 10,000 feet in the Colorado Rockies. I slowly moved undetected to within 60 yards of the bull. I didn't want to chance getting any closer, but heavy underbrush blocked the chest cavity, so I grunted a few times and the bull stood, offering a perfect broadside shot. I held my sights as steady as I ever had…then eased back on the trigger. The sound of the percussion cap and powder charge exploding sounded as one, and I heard the sound of that soft lead ball driving home.

As if not even hit, that bull stiff legged it out of that pocket and was still going a half-mile away. Then, I noticed him falter, and immediately slow to head-down walk. I reloaded and quickly covered the distance, and when I eased up to the thicket into which I had watched the elk disappear, there he stood 50 yards away. I could see the first hit, and it looked good. So, I held for the same spot and shot again. This time the bull half fell, then caught himself and walked another 200 yards before going down. Both of the lead balls had passed through both lungs, and were recovered almost side by side in the opposite rib cage.

At 60 yards, my mighty fifty-caliber round ball rifle had hit that bull with just under 1,000 f.p.e., and it still took another duplicate shot from 50 yards to get the job done. But not before that elk had traveled more than a half-mile. The same load had brought down every whitetail shot with the rifle within 40 yards of where the deer were standing, and the two 300-pound wild hogs and the bear went down on the spot. Yet, that 600-pound bull elk had to be shot twice, and each time it traveled a fair distance before stopping. Fortunately, the country was extremely open, and I could visually watch the bull's route both times.

On another elk hunt in the Wasatch Range of northern Utah some 20 years later, one frosty morning I found myself watching the approach of a huge 900-pound 6x5 bull my hunting partner had bugled up from a deep canyon. When that elk turned broadside at about 60 yards, I held just to the rear of the front shoulder, and eased back on the trigger. However, instead of shooting a longer-barreled traditional-styled side-hammer loaded with a patched round ball, this time I was using a very modern Knight .50 caliber in-line loaded with 110 grains of Pyrodex RS/Select and a saboted 300-grain all-copper Barnes Expander MZ hollow-point. And when that projectile drove home, at just about the same spot where I had placed my shots on my very first bull two decades earlier, that bull didn't cover a half-mile before stopping. Instead, the elk ran hard for about 50 yards, stopped abruptly, and took several steps backward before flipping over.

At the muzzle, the load was good for about 1,600 f.p.s. and 1,700 f.p.e., basically the same muzzle energy level developed by the patched round ball load in my custom Leman full-stock. However, the cylindrical Barnes bullet has far better aerodynamics than a lead sphere, and at 60 yards the 300-grain bullet had not slowed much. In fact, Barnes lists the ballistic coefficient of the bullet at .207, which means that at a 1,600 f.p.s. muzzle velocity, the bullet would still be moving at around 1,350 f.p.s. and hitting with a little over 1,200 f.p.e. at 100 yards. My big Utah bull was hit with close to 1,500 pounds of punch at 60 yards.

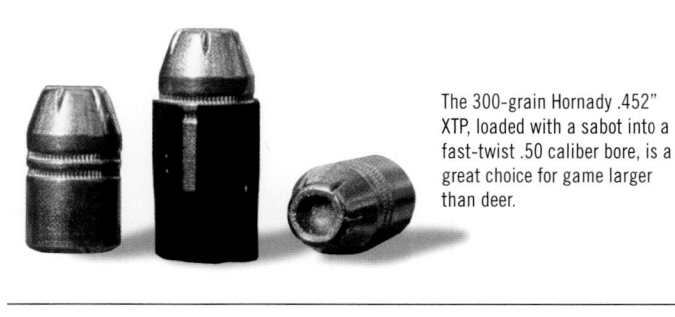

The 300-grain Hornady .452" XTP, loaded with a sabot into a fast-twist .50 caliber bore, is a great choice for game larger than deer.

The difference in the performance of the two loads, the two entirely different projectiles for the two different .50 caliber rifles was literally as different as night and day. Simply put, the old patched round ball just doesn't cut it as a big game projectile, especially when the game being hunted could top a half-ton in weight. Still, a few game departments such as that in Colorado and Oregon continue to show their ignorance of muzzleloader performance by continuing to allow the use of the patched round ball on elk-sized game, while outlawing the use of far superior saboted bullets like the Barnes Expander MZ.

It is way past due for serious muzzleloading hunters to make these game departments accountable for such decisions. Likewise, it's time to establish minimum allowable energy levels (based on remaining energy at 100 yards) for hunting elk, moose, caribou and a few other larger-sized species of big game. Not many round ball loads would make the cut if a load had to hit with no less than 1,000 foot-pounds at 100 yards.

Even a .54 caliber rifle loaded with 140 grains of Pyrodex "RS/Select" behind a patched 220-grain .530" round ball would fail to meet this criteria. At the muzzle of a 28-inch barrel, the load would get the ball out of the barrel at around 1,895 f.p.s. And at the muzzle, the 220-grain ball would have right at 1,750 f.p.e. However, by the time that ball hit the 100-yard mark, velocity would be down to around 1,130 f.p.s. and that ball would hit a fine bull elk with less than 650 foot-pounds of energy. Hardly a potent load for game this big, but allowed in every elk hunting state.

When it comes to generating big-game-taking energy levels, today's modern in-line rifles are impossible to beat, whether they are loaded with a heavy

North American wild sheep can top 400 pounds in weight. Wildlife photographer Mike Pelligatti used his Knight MK-85 to take this beautiful ram at almost 200 yards. He was shooting a saboted 300-grain Hornady XTP bullet.

saboted bullet or a modern bore-sized conical bullet. I have been a big proponent of the saboted bullets ever since I began shooting them during the mid-1980s. I feel that the sabot system better allows a hunter to tailor his loads for the game being hunted, and I have shot a wide range of big game with my in-line muzzle-loaders with bullets from as light as 175 grains up to 325 grains. For game as large as elk, and larger, I've come to lean in favor of bullets of at least 300 grains.

However, before going to saboted bullets, I hunted almost exclusively with the bore-sized heavy lead conical bullets out of the .50 caliber rifles I preferred. One of my favorites was the 385-grain hollow-base, hollow-point conical bullet from Buffalo Bullet Company. This bullet proved exceptionally accurate out of a custom .50 caliber half-stock I built during the early 1980s, using a fast (for the time anyway) one turn-in-24 inches rifled bore. With a 100-grain charge of Py-rodex "RS," the scoped side-hammer would consistently print the big soft lead con-ical bullet inside of 3 inches at 100 yards, and I took a lot of game with that rifle. Of course, that was before I met Tony Knight in late 1985, and was ruined forever by the effectiveness of a modern in-line rifle and the saboted bullets I would come to prefer.

Gary "Doc" White has built an excellent reputation for the effectiveness of his White Rifles loaded with big heavy lead conical bullets. Currently, the company only offers their in-line models in .45, .50 and .54 caliber. However, at one time, White also offered several models in .40 caliber as well, but the smaller bore size just did not enjoy the widespread popularity needed to keep it in the line-up. This was mainly due to the fact that in most states, the .40 caliber could not be legally used to hunt game even the size of whitetail deer, and especially anything larger. White continues to offer the most popular bullet for the .40 caliber rifles they once sold, and that's a long 400-grain (.409" diameter) PowerPunch bullet. Loaded with a 100-grain charge of Pyrodex "P," a .40 caliber White Rifle could get the bullet out of the muzzle at around 1,400 f.p.s. Now, that translates into 1,740 f.p.e. This very long, smaller diameter, projectile is extremely aerodynamic in flight, and at 100 yards the bullet would still hit with more than 1,300 f.p.e.—or, more than enough to cleanly harvest game as large as elk or even moose.

Isn't it odd that a game department would prohibit the use of such a rifle and load, but still permit the use of a larger .54 caliber loaded with a round ball that hits with only about half that amount of energy at 100 yards?

Like I said, it's time for serious muzzleloading hunters to tell the game departments what works and what doesn't. They surely don't know.

Doc White has taken just about every species of North American game with rifles of his design, plus an impressive list of African and Asian big game. Of all the game he's hunted, he rates a huge near 3,000-pound Asian water buffalo he shot a couple of years back as one of the toughest and most orneriest beasts he's ever hunted with a muzzleloader. For the hunt, he used a .50 caliber White rifle, loaded with a 140-grain charge of Pyrodex "P" behind one of the company's massive 600-grain PowerPunch bullets. Gary says the load is good for 1,400 f.p.s., and develops right at 2,600 f.p.e. He shot the bull at about 90 yards when it offered a perfect broadside shot. The big bullet passed through both lungs and lodged, expanded to more than quarter-size diameter, against the rib cage on the opposite side. The huge bull went only a few yards before going down.

More and more, muzzleloading hunters are going after game that was once reserved only for those who hunted with a very large bore center-fire rifle, like the .458 Winchester Magnum or .460 Weatherby Magnum. With the right powder charge and proper bullet selection, the muzzleloading hunter who takes the time to work up an accurate load will find that the majority of the high performance muzzleloading big game rifles now available can be loaded for game as big as moose—or even bigger.

Thanks to the efficiency and knockdown power delivered by today's modern in-line ignition muzzleloading big game rifles, hunters are now relying on these guns and loads to hunt all over the world.

ever changing muzzleloading
REGULATIONS

FAR RIGHT: The in-line rifle, saboted bullet load and scope sight combination used by legendary turkey call maker Dale Rohm to take this nice buck would have been illegal in a vast majority of states during the late 1980s. Today, it can be used during the vast majority of muzzleloader hunting seasons.

If you could step back in time 20 or so years, you would be surprised at how much more restrictive muzzleloader hunting regulations were during the mid- to late 1980s. Up until that point, muzzleloading had remained pretty well an extremely traditional-oriented shooting and hunting sport. And when the first modern-looking Knight MK-85 in-line rifles and the Muzzleload Magnum Products plastic sabots appeared on the scene in the mid 1980s, those muzzleloading innovations created an uproar among shooters and hunters with a strong traditional mind-set.

Across the country, traditional muzzleloader shooters banded together to fight the modernization of the sport. Just about everywhere, statewide muzzleloading associations flocked to game department meetings to get the newfangled guns and loads banned from use during the special muzzleloader seasons. The accuracy and efficiency of the new in-line rifles and loads built around a modern jacketed hollow-point bullet gripped by a plastic sabot seemed to threaten the sport these shooters loved so dearly. And with the immediate opposition, the future of advanced muzzleloading rifle and load technology didn't look too bright.

Within a couple of years, in-line rifles had been singled out and made illegal for use during the special muzzleloader seasons in nearly a dozen states, while saboted handgun or pistol bullets were regulated against in even more states. At first, even the rest of the muzzleloading rifle industry turned against a fledgling Modern Muzzleloading, Inc., which made and marketed the Knight in-line rifles. Companies like Thompson/Center Arms openly lobbied against the legalization of in-line ignition rifles, and even stated in their owner's manual that if a shooter loaded and fired a bullet with a plastic patch (sabot) of any type, the warranty on that rifle would be void.

Modern technology had stepped into the muzzleloading arena and the "Chicken Littles" among us sincerely felt that the modernization of the sport would prove detrimental to the further establishment of muzzleloader hunting opportunities. Their "We'll lose our muzzleloading seasons!…We'll lose our muzzleloading seasons!" cries could be heard from coast to coast, from north to south. But, have we lost one muzzleloader hunting opportunity or season to the acceptance of modern in-line rifles…to the widespread use of plastic saboted bullets…to the legalization of telescopic sights…or due to the development of advanced muzzleloader propellants? The answer is, "No, we haven't!"

The Knight MK-85 in-line rifle's very modern lines and looks once caused traditional-minded muzzleloading shooters to rise up against modernization of the sport.

In fact, all these modern influences have had just the opposite effect on muzzleloader hunting. Today, there are an estimated 3.5 million muzzleloading gun owners in this country, and at one time or another most of them hunt with these front-loaders. During the early 1980s, the number of muzzleloading shooters in the United States was right at 1 million. What brought all of these new shooters, and hunters, into the sport? It wasn't the nostalgia of mastering an old-fashioned front-loading design from the past. It was the lure of the bonus hunting offered by the special muzzleloader seasons—and the new guns and loads that allowed them to cleanly harvest big game.

During the past couple of decades, no other hunting regulations have undergone as much change as those that govern the use of a muzzle-loaded big game rifle. Today, in-lines of one type or another can be hunted with in every state. Saboted bullets are now legal in all but a couple of states. And telescopic sights are now allowed in nearly 75 percent of all states. Muzzleloading has definitely become a true hunting sport, and the changes in what is a legal muzzleloader now simply reflect the wishes of those who participate in these special seasons or hunts.

For years, the most restrictive muzzleloading season in the country was the flintlock only season in Pennsylvania. The hunt took place in December, after the general firearms season, and when the weather could be at its worse. To cash in on another opportunity to put some venison in the freezer, the season, at first anyway, was extremely popular. During the mid-1980s, as many as 140,000 Pennsylvania hunters flocked to the deer woods—with flintlock in hand. Then the inefficiency of the flint-and-steel ignition system began to take its toll as hunters grew weary of not being able to make a good shot with a gun that only a true flintlock-shooting purist could master. By the early 1990s, the number of hunters participating in this season had dwindled to only about 60,000. And even though the Pennsylvania Game Commission wanted an increased doe harvest for management reasons, the flintlock muzzleloading season in this state enjoyed only about an 8 percent success rate.

In 2001, the state of Pennsylvania began to listen to the wants and needs of the muzzleloading hunters in that state and established an entirely new muzzle-

The introduction of modern technology to muzzleloader hunting has regularly seen strong opposition from followers of historical muzzleloading, who enjoy reliving history through the guns they shoot and hunt with. Today, those who hunt with authentically styled guns from the 1700s and early 1800s represent less than 10 percent of all muzzleloader hunters.

loading season in October, before the opener of the modern firearms season. And this new season permits just about *ANY* muzzleloaded rifle, with very few restrictions on the type of ignition, type of projectile, type of sighting system or the type of propellant used. The result has been a very successful turnaround for the state. Hunters now get to go afield with the latest in muzzleloading technology, and the game department is now getting the doe harvest needed to get a grasp on a burgeoning deer population.

Not all is rosy when it comes to muzzleloading regulations in all states. The Colorado muzzleloader seasons for elk and mule deer are among the most popular seasons in the country today. Unfortunately, the game department here listens too closely to the wants and wishes of the Colorado State Muzzleloading Association, a very historical-driven organization made up of fewer than 200 members statewide. Yet, when the game commission holds its meetings, members of this organization show up and lobby against further modernization of the guns and loads allowed during the muzzleloader only hunts. Their influence has caused the

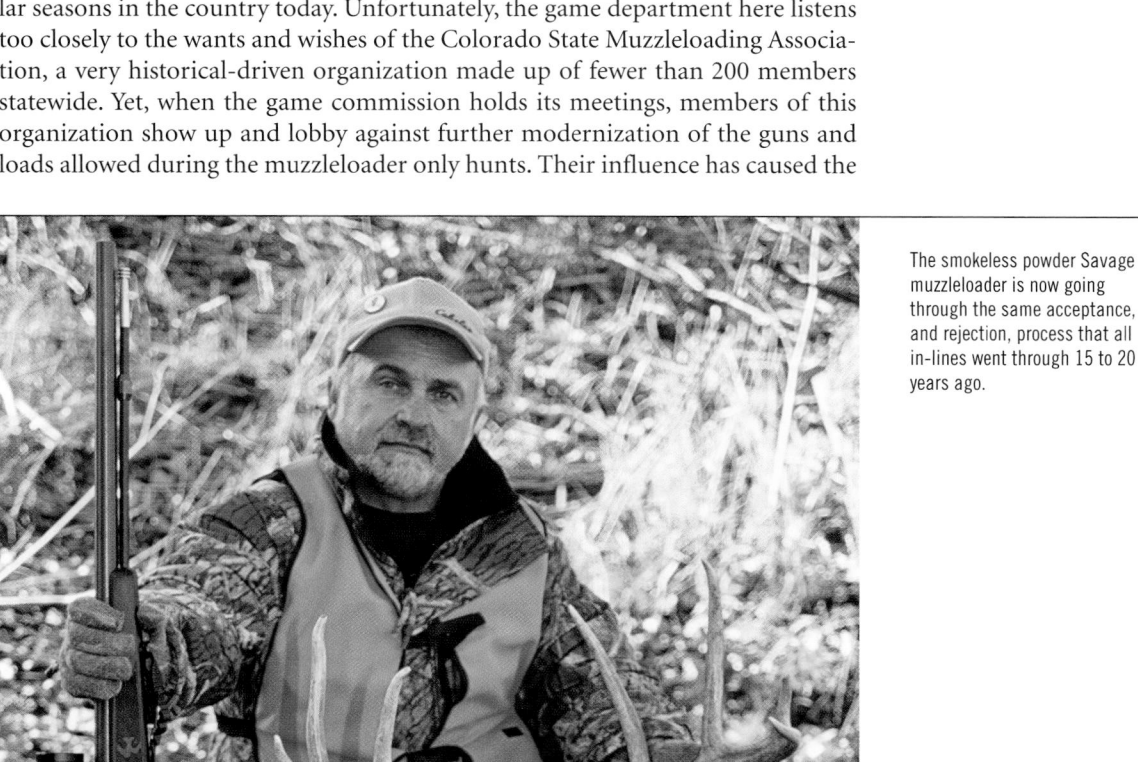

The smokeless powder Savage muzzleloader is now going through the same acceptance, and rejection, process that all in-lines went through 15 to 20 years ago.

Colorado Division of Wildlife to ban the use of in-line rifles several times since the late 1980s. Fortunately, when the muzzleloading hunters who actually make up the 40,000 or so such hunters that go after big game with a muzzleloader each season began to speak out, the game department rescinded those bands—both times.

Colorado regulations still continue to be among the most antiquated in the country. Hunters here are not allowed to shoot saboted bullets. Pelletized charges of Pyrodex or Triple Seven are not permitted. Conical bullets cannot be more than twice as long as they are in diameter. And telescopic sights cannot be used during the special muzzleloader seasons. Other states with ridiculous restrictions that dictate the rifle and load that can be legally used include Oregon, Washington and Idaho. All three of these states have regulations in place that make it impossible to hunt with a modern in-line rifle that uses a superior rifle or shotgun primer for more sure-fire ignition, or allow the use of a scope. Plus in Oregon, hunters can only use either a patched round ball or bore-sized concial bullet for hunting big

Today's muzzleloading hunter wants to bring down the game being hunted as cleanly and humanely as possible. It seems odd that some state muzzleloading regulations force the use of a less than optimum rifle, powder charge, projectile or sighting system.

game during the muzzleloader seasons. And a legal conical bullet cannot have a plastic skirt attached like that on the popular Power Belt bullets.

A number of states currently do not permit the use of modern smokeless powders in the Savage Model 10ML II during the muzzleloader seasons. However, this will begin to change as the benefits of shooting smokeless powders in this rifle, and other smokeless designs that are sure to follow, are realized by the hunters who use them. And still, a full 25 percent of all states continue to ban the use of magnifying optics on a muzzle-loaded big game rifle.

Why? Are these game managers afraid that a hunter just might cleanly kill outright the game they're shooting at? But, isn't that the idea? Most responsible big game hunters work hard to develop a load that can do the job, and then spend many hours at the bench every year to refine their shooting ability. Once a hunter has decided to shoot an animal, isn't it ethical to do it as cleanly as possible? Well, that becomes increasingly difficult when regulations such as those in effect in Colorado, Oregon, Washington, Idaho and a number of other states throw up regulatory hurdles that make the rifles and loads being hunted with less effective than they could be.

Game departments do not make the regulations. Each of you makes the regulations. And if enough of you get together and force the game departments to change outdated muzzleloading regulations, it then becomes their job to figure out how to make it all work. Today, traditional muzzleloading shooters make up only about 10 percent of all muzzleloading hunters in the country. Yet they have

more influence with the game departments than the 90 percent who like some modern technology in the guns and loads they hunt with. And that's because traditional-minded organizations in most states enjoy some organization, while hunters do not. If you want change in regulations which dictate the use of a muzzle-loaded rifle and load that's less effective than what's being used in most states these days, all muzzleloader hunters must become better organized. Change is possible if all performance-minded hunters work together to counter the influence of those who would like to keep muzzleloading in the dark ages.

TOP: In open country like this, wouldn't a scope make sense? Not if regulations prohibit its use. Close to 25 percent of the states still do not allow the use of telescopic sights.

BOTTOM: Colorado offers some of the finest muzzleloader big game hunting in the country. Unfortunately, the game department imposes some very antiquated muzzleloading regulations that prohibit scopes, pelletized powder charges and efficient saboted bullets.

muzzleloading into
THE FUTURE

Back when I made the decision to become a muzleloading hunter at the ripe old age of 13, there was no way I could have ever envisioned the guns…the loads…the performance many of us take for granted today. Nor would I have ever guessed that, some day, the vast majority of states from coast to coast would offer the dedicated big game hunter special muzzleloader only hunting seasons.

The road that muzzleloading has traveled the past 50 or so years has definitely been a bumpy one. Every time any new product that came to the market strayed too far from what was accepted at the time, muzzleloading shooters tended to initially reject it. They seemed to resent change. There was resistance to using a conical bullet over the older patched round ball…the thought of shooting the "replica black powder" known as Pyrodex during the mid- to late 1970s turned many against further modernization of the sport…and when Tony Knight introduced his MK-85 in-line rifles nearly 20 years ago, there was a nationwide movement to get the rifles banned—mostly because of their ultramodern looks.

There is one thing that no one could have ever accused the typical traditional-minded muzzleloading shooter of the 1970s and 1980s of being—and that was being open-minded. Fortunately, through the persistence of those who brought new innovations to the market, and to overall improved designs, these and many other modern-oriented products managed to hang on until the serious muzzleloading hunter repeatedly experienced the vastly improved performance of the new guns, new powders and new bullets on big game. And as the ranks of this new breed of muzzleloading shooter grew rapidly, companies that refused to meet the wants and needs of the modern-day muzzleloading hunter vanished from the marketplace.

FAR LEFT: Keeping the muzzleloading market alive and vibrant with exciting new products will encourage hunters to spend money on new muzzleloading guns and accessories, boosting the economy at several levels.

BELOW: As long as we have a healthy big game population, a healthy muzzleloading industry, and a continued interest in hunting, the sport of hunting big game with a muzzle-loaded rifle should enjoy a bright future.

Communities that not only accept hunting but embrace it openly stand to benefit from the dollars hunters spend annually, including those who hunt with a muzzle-loaded rifle.

With the growing interest in hunting deer and other big game with a muzzleloader, several million muzzleloading hunters nationwide provide needed conservation dollars through permits purchased.

For muzzleloading, change has been good. The easier it has become to get the velocity, the energy and the accuracy needed to accomplish the absolute best job of cleanly harvesting a big game animal, the more muzzleloading has attracted new followers from the ranks of both modern gun and archery hunters. Likewise, game departments have responded to the growing numbers of muzzleloading hunters by establishing new muzzleloader hunting seasons, which, in turn, have attracted still more participants.

So, where is muzzleloading headed another 20 or 30 years down that road, and what will affect the future growth of this sport?

Many knowledgeable muzzleloading experts in the industry have acknowledged that three basic things will shape the future of this 700-year-old shooting sport. First, the health of the big game populations is the most important factor. Whitetail populations are still growing in a few areas of the country, while the herds have stabilized, for the moment anyway, in other areas. Fortunately, the numbers of whitetail deer haven't really dwindled in too many areas. Overall, the numbers of these deer are at all-time highs in just about every region of the country. And this is why muzzleloader hunting enjoys such popularity in just about every state where whitetails are hunted. Compared to the bag limits imposed on deer 25 years ago, today's hunter can now harvest two…three…four or more times as many deer. And many of these deer are now being taken with muzzle-loaded rifles.

The next most important factor is the health of the muzzleloading market itself. All shooting sports need new and more exciting products on a regular basis to stay alive, and muzzleloading is certainly no exception. Product sales stimulate the economy, and the muzzleloading hunter who purchases a new front-loader every few years, or regularly tries the newest powders and bullets to find a better performing load helps to finance the development of still better products in the future. Not to mention that such sales help to keep local gun shops in business. Also, a state that caters to the muzzleloader hunter stands to benefit monetarily, through permit sales and through lodging, dining and travel costs. And don't forget guide fees or the money spent on hunting leases.

Third, the interest in hunting with a muzzleloader has to be maintained. Most agree that as long as we have a healthy big game population and the regular introduction of exciting new muzzleloading guns and accessories, there will always be hunter interest. True, but there are a few negative factors that tend to chill hunter enthusiasm.

Go back to Chapter 4 and take a look at the sidebar that deals with "The High Cost of High Performance." Shooting almost any of today's better performing modern in-line muzzleloading rifles has gotten expensive—too expensive! As pointed out, you can actually shoot a big African dangerous game rifle like the .458 Winchester Magnum more economically than you can a number of today's high performance front-loaders. When manufacturers develop a rifle around the use of special loading aids, a specific nonstandard bullet and exclusive sabot, primarily with the intention of charging much higher than usual prices for these components, they are taking advantage of the consumer. And when the rifle requires a costly powder charge to tap its performance, the cost per shot can go sky high. And when the cost of shooting such a rifle gets so high that the owner rarely takes it to the range, it just might also become his last choice to use during any hunt.

The future of muzzleloader hunting is partially driven by the introduction of new products, like the innovative "The Bullet," a saboted muzzleloading projectile that has a hole running through its center.

In recent years, the bickering over muzzleloader development has continued. Only now, it's not so much between the muzzleloading shooters and hunters. It is now between those manufacturers who bring us all of those great new rifles and muzzleloader hunting products.

When promoting the effectiveness of today's high performance muzzleloading big game rifles, it has become a game of one-upmanship between muzzleloading rifle makers. No one wants to tout anything other than the fastest velocity...highest energy levels...or flattest trajectory. And some of the ballistics claims by more than a few have crossed over into the realm of make-believe! (But then, most consumers don't own a chronograph to check velocities, or have the means to translate those velocities with a given bullet weight into the energy produced.) And when a manufacturer comes to the market with a product that is clearly superior to anything else out there, competing makers have learned to revert to another tactic. And that's to lobby for legislation to get regulations passed that would prohibit that product's use during the special muzzleloader seasons.

Why do you think there is this constant push for revised muzzleloader hunting regulations? Muzzleloading went high performance 20 years ago, and state regulations continue to change each and every year in one state or another— usually to ban this or that, or to allow new products by those manufacturers with the strongest lobbying powers. Caught in the middle of all this is the consumer, who becomes afraid to buy the newest and latest products in fear that the game department in his or her state may get pressured to make its use illegal.

Muzzleloading is big business. Every year between 300,000 and 400,000 muzzle-loaded guns are sold in North America. At an average retail price of $300, that's $90,000,000 to $120,000,000 in sales. Add to that the sales of muzzleloader bullets, sabots, percussion caps, powders and a wide range of accessories, and you are looking at a $250,000,000 to $300,000,000 market annually. And everyone in the business wants to take another's piece of the pie away.

But, competition has been good for the market, as well as for the growth of muzzleloader hunting. And with so much good to enjoy, we'll just have to accept a little bad.

Despite the fierce competition among muzzleloading rifle manufacturers, ever changing muzzleloading regulations and the high cost of shooting today's top-performing in-line rifles, the future still looks bright for hunting with a muzzleloader. The only thing constant about the sport we all love so dearly has been change. And out of all that has changed through the past 50 years has evolved the guns, loads and hunting opportunities enjoyed today. Hopefully, future changes will prove just as beneficial.

Much of the Midwest is heavy agricultural land, where the use of center-fire deer rifles continues to be curtailed with each new season. Today's super accurate "one-shot" in-line muzzleloaders are fully capable of cleanly harvesting whitetails out to and slightly past 200 yards.

Interest in muzzleloader big game hunting is slowly beginning to spread to hunting other species as well. The author took this big ol' Iowa tom with a muzzle-loaded Knight MK-85 in-line shotgun.

A lot of water has gone under the bridge since William "Tony" Knight introduced the first successful in-line percussion hunting rifle—the MK-85. His design opened the door to the modernization of this sport, appealing to a larger segment of the hunting crowd. Today, one deer in five or six is harvested with a muzzle-loaded rifle.

And out of all that has changed through the past 50 years has evolved the guns, loads and hunting opportunities enjoyed today.